ANALYSING COMMUNITY WORK

ITS THEORY AND PRACTICE

Keith Popple

OPEN UNIVERSITY PRESS
Buckingham · Philadelphia

Open University Press
Celtic Court
22 Ballmoor
Buckingham
MK18 1XW

and
1900 Frost Road, Suite 101
Bristol, PA 19007, USA

First published 1995
Reprinted 1996, 1997

A catalogue record of this book is available from the British Library

ISBN 0 335 19408 7 (pb)   0 335 19409 5 (hb)

Library of Congress Cataloging-in-Publication Data
Popple, Keith.
    Analysing community work: its theory and practice / Keith Popple.
        p.   cm.
    Includes bibliographical references and index.
    ISBN 0–335–19409–5 ISBN 0–335–19408–7 (pbk.)
    1. Social service—Great Britain.   2. Community organization–
–Great Britain.   I. Title.
HV245.P65   1995
361.8'0941—dc20   95–6959

Typeset by Graphicraft Typesetters Ltd, Hong Kong
Printed and bound in Great Britain by
Biddles Ltd, Guildford and King's Lynn

ANALYSING COMMUNITY WORK

ITS THEORY AND PRACTICE

For Daniel

CONTENTS

	Acknowledgements	ix
Chapter 1	Introduction	1
Chapter 2	The development of British community work	7
Chapter 3	Community work theory	31
Chapter 4	Community work theory: the way forward?	43
Chapter 5	Models of community work	54
Chapter 6	Community work in practice	74
Chapter 7	Conclusion and future directions	96
	References	105
Appendix A	Select Community Development Project bibliography	123
Appendix B	Job categories where community work training units could be of relevance	125
	Index	127

ACKNOWLEDGEMENTS

I would like to acknowledge and express my gratitude to the many people who have made a contribution in one way or another to the production of this book.

Several cohorts of students on the BSc (Hons) Social Policy and Administration plus Diploma in Community Work at the University of Plymouth have experienced my attempts to work on the book while teaching and engaging with them in some of the ideas offered in it. Their feedback has been helpful. Similarly, I would like to record my appreciation for the encouragement given to me by staff in the Department of Applied Social Science, University of Plymouth. I am especially grateful for the contribution the late Phil Bashford made to my thinking on community work. He is greatly missed.

My thanks are extended to a large number of people including Robin Means who offered his time and thoughts at different stages. Numerous people have suggested ideas and material for the book, including Val Harris of the Association of Community Workers and Hazel Morbey. I also wish to acknowledge the encouragement given by Gary Craig, Marg Mayo, Tony Jeffs, Chris Miller and Ruth Lister.

This book reflects my work and discussions with many community workers. I am particularly grateful to all the staff at Barton Hill Settlement in Bristol and Virginia House Settlement in Plymouth for sharing experiences of their work.

Thanks also go to all the staff at the Open University Press who have worked diligently to produce this volume, in particular Jacinta Evans who encouraged me to translate my ideas into a book. I am also grateful for the unstinting work of Sharon Ward who typed the manuscript.

My heartfelt thanks also go out to my family and friends who have supported me in my enterprise.

Finally, I would like to say a big 'thank you' to Daniel who has patiently waited for me to play and read with him, to take and collect him from school, and to cook and look after him while I was juggling with completing my writing. This book is for him.

Chapter *1*

INTRODUCTION

Community work is an area of practice that is both imprecise and unclear. It can be almost everything (or anything) to everyone. Yet community work *is* a particular activity with clear boundaries and target groups. It *is* informed by a range of disciplines that clearly place the activity in the education and welfare fields. It is also undertaken by practitioners who are clear what they should and should not do. Community work, then, is a contradictory activity that suffers from being under-theorized and under-researched. It is both exciting and yet frustrating for those who want to know more about it and, more importantly, want to understand it so that they can practise more effectively.

This book is an attempt to make a small contribution to the knowledge base and debate within the field of community work by clarifying its constituent themes. The book has evolved from the problem I have encountered as a practitioner and now as a teacher of community work when looking for appropriate texts. I have found, like others, a paucity of literature to assist and understand the activity's theory and practice. The community work literature that is available, particularly that from projects, is frequently descriptive and often anecdotal. This is underlined by a view that community work is experimental and not a permanent area of work. This book therefore aims to locate community work within a theoretical base, and as an important and useful activity. Overall, it is my hope that the book will help to sharpen community work's critical edge, to increase its critical analysis, and to assist in its practice.

What is community?

The evolving sociological debates surrounding the term community have been well documented (Abrams, 1978; Bell and Newby, 1971; Black, 1988; Clark, 1983; Cornwell, 1984; Fraser, 1987; Golding and Sills, 1983; Pahl, 1966; Stacey, 1969; Thorns, 1976; Wilmott, 1963, 1989; Wilmott and Thomas, 1984). For instance, Bell and Newby (1971) found 98 different definitions of the term, while Abrams (1978: 11) succinctly declared that

the concept of community for its part is slowly being evicted from British sociology, not because there is agreement on the empirical collapse of community, but rather because the term has come to be used so variously and different relationships, identified as those of community, have been discovered in so many different contexts that the word itself has become almost devoid of precise meaning.

It is not my purpose here to pursue another definition, rather to highlight some differing understandings that reflect this imprecision and contentiousness.

The dominant view of community is an idealized one which always locates a 'golden age' of clearly defined and secure neighbourhoods in the historical period before the present one. This is a recurring theme in British people's understanding of their own history which is examined by Pearson (1983) in relation to street crime and hooliganism. The traditional view also represents community as a place of warmth, intimacy and social cohesion. The German sociologist Ferdinand Tönnies (1955) has influenced the dominant view of community with his distinction between two kinds of social relationship. One is based on affection, kinship, or membership of a community, such as a family or a group of friends. To describe this Tönnies used the German word *Gemeinschaft*. The other kind of social relationship is based upon the division of labour and contractual relations between isolated individuals consulting only their own self-interest. Tönnies referred to this society as *Gesellschaft*. Although Tönnies's terms need to be viewed as mental constructs, or ideal types, and do not correspond to any existing society, they do carry with it the suggestion that Western civilization is passing through the predominance of *Gemeinschaft* to a state of *Gesellschaft*. The implication given is that many of the problems within contemporary society are due to this change. The term community in this paradigm contains associations which are often connected with security and nostalgic notions of childhood and have been used to effect in a great deal of popular literature and television 'soap operas'. Two long-running examples of the latter include *Coronation Street*, which portrays a Lancashire urban working-class community, and *Emmerdale*, which is set in a rural community in the Yorkshire Dales.

The concept of community for romantic socialists like William Morris (1887; 1918) (see also Meier, 1978; Thompson, 1977) and John Ruskin (for discussions on the work of Ruskin see Anthony, 1983; Rosenberg, 1961), for G.D.H. Cole's guild socialist utopia (Cole, 1918; 1920) and, until fairly recently, for certain sections of the Labour Party (Beilharz, 1992), must also be approached with caution. Such a view of community has been drawn from a nostalgic picture of working-class culture that is allegedly built on sound, deeply bedded socialist principles which are waiting for the order to march behind the accredited leader of the day. With some notable exceptions (for example, Cockburn, 1977; Craig et al., 1982), Marxists have historically ignored the role of community in the scheme of sites for struggle, preferring instead to concentrate on social production.

The dominant and the romantic socialist concepts of community typify the problem of securing an agreed definition, although Williams (1976: 66) claims the term is rarely used disparagingly:

> Community can be the warmly persuasive word to describe an existing set of relationships, or the warmly persuasive word to describe an alternative set of relationships. What is most important, perhaps, is that unlike all other terms of social organization (state, nation, society etc.) it never seems to be used unfavourably, and never to be given any positive opposing or distinguishing term.

In contrast, the term community has come under scrutiny and criticism from the radical left. This was particularly so in the late 1970s. Cockburn (1977) and Cowley et al. (1977) dismiss the concept as one used by the state itself – for example, in the titling of state services: community schools, community police officers, community nurses and so on. These critics claim that the term community hides the nature of powerful forces ranged against each other – the working class and the capitalist class. Cockburn (1977: 163) states that the concept of community should highlight the reproduction of labour power that is mediated within communities: 'what we are involved in is struggle in the field of capitalistic reproduction'. Political and economic struggles, in her view, take place in the workplace, in schools, on the streets, and in families. Community workers can, according to Cockburn, emphasize that 'community' often means 'family' or more strictly 'women' (see also Wilson, 1977). We shall be returning to the importance of women's role in the community at different stages of the book. Further, the traditional views of community have failed to recognize the ethnically diverse make-up of many neighbourhoods. The 1991 Census (OPCS, 1993a) indicates that black people form 5.5% of the total population; and closer examination reveals that they are concentrated in particular geographical areas. For instance, 20.2% of the Greater London population is black (OPCS, 1993b).

There has been a recent addition to the literature on community intervention by Butcher et al. (1993) who offer a view that community can be a positive site for a broad range of approaches and concepts. Providing both descriptive reflections and analytical examinations of the relationship between public policy and community values, the writers suggest a communitarian vision that recognizes communities' limitations and strengths.

We can see that definitions of community are elusive, imprecise, contradictory and controversial. Community has both descriptive and evaluative meanings, and is as much an ideological construct as a description of a locality. The term not only exists in a geographical and material sense but also reflects people's thinking and feeling as to where they believe a community exists. Thus other than elucidating the concept through its examination, one operational definition may be that community exists in three broad categories, as discussed by Wilmott (1989: 2). One is defined in terms of locality or territory; another as a communality of interest or interest group such as the black community or Jewish community; the third, a group composed of people sharing a common condition or problem such as alcohol dependency or cancer, or a common bond such as working for the same employer. Although this is a useful categorization, community must remain an essentially contested concept.

The definition of community is important to community work theory and practice because, as we will uncover, this indicates a theoretical position. One perception of community work is that it takes place in a pluralist society (and therefore in pluralist communities) and upon the premise of heterogeneity and inter-group competition. An opposing view perceives community work as taking place within communities and in a society that is based upon conflict and on the premise of class structure, inequality and powerlessness.

What is community work?

The term community work is likewise a contested concept and there is no universally agreed meaning. The fluidity in its definition presents particular problems and challenges for a book of this kind which will become apparent in later chapters. However, it is useful at this stage to draw together briefly some of the major competing views that constitute the central debates on contemporary practice. This debate is further examined in Chapter 3 which explores the theories informing community work.

An understanding of community work can be related to political values. Since the 1960s community work theory and practice have been influenced by two macro theories: the pluralist; and the radical and socialist.

The pluralist approach has dominated community work theory and practice since the early 1960s and is expounded in the writings of, among others, Goetschius (1969; 1975), Thomas (1978; 1980; 1983) and Twelvetrees (1976; 1991). Pluralism is a political perspective that attaches major significance to pressure groups and interest groups in which, its advocates claim, are centres of power and influence. It is believed for instance, that in the United Kingdom a multiple of interest groups, such as religious groups, trade unions, political parties, pressure groups and black groups, share power with central government. It is argued that there is a balance in these competing interests so that all, in different ways, have some impact upon policy, but none dominates the mechanism of government. One advocate of pluralist theories in community work, Thomas, suggests two major elements to the activity: the 'distributive' and the 'developmental'. Thomas is sceptical of radical and socialist theories, and practice that is overly political. Instead, he believes that only small-scale change is possible, or desirable, and stresses the educational and experimental aspects of the work.

Critical of the pluralist model of community work for its negation of a wider political analysis, the Community Development Project literature (see Appendix A for a selected bibliography), Craig et al. (1982), Dominelli (1990), Forrest (1984), Jacobs (1984; 1994), Lees and Mayo (1984) and Sayer (1986), among several, develop models of theory and practice based on radical and socialist principles. These writers place community work within a struggle for macro change, many developing ideas that incorporate the experiences of community action and the labour movement. Jacobs (1984), for instance, argues that socialism needs to re-establish its relationship with working-class communities and believes it can do so by examining the lessons learnt from radical community work. Similarly, Craig et al. (1982) attempt to develop a radical theoretical base for community work practice. These conflict-focused perspectives have similarly addressed issues of race (Mullard, 1973; Ohri et al., 1982; Sondhi, 1994) and sex equality (Curno et al., 1982; Dominelli and McLeod, 1989; Flynn et al., 1986; Dominelli, 1994; Rogers, 1994) within community work. The theme of these discussions has been to recognize a disparate experience within communities and the need to tackle structured inequalities at the neighbourhood level.

These two main perspectives, together with the influence of theories from feminism, and the black and anti-racist critique, will be examined and evaluated in greater depth in Chapter 3. Chapter 4 will offer an emerging understanding of community work based upon broader theoretical perspectives.

Against often conflicting values and goals for community work it is difficult to provide a hard definition of the term. However, a statement which offers us a useful starting point in our consideration is that given by Taylor and Presley (1987: 2).

> Community work is not a profession like any other. It is a profession dedicated to increasing the expertise of non-professionals; to increasing the capacity of people in difficult and disadvantaged situations, getting more control over their collective circumstances. Community workers stimulate and support groups of people working to improve conditions and opportunities in their own neighbourhoods. The immediate aims are often concrete – better amenities, housing, job-opportunities; the underlying aim is an increase in confidence, skill and community self-organizing power which will enable the participants to continue to use and spread these abilities long after the community worker has gone.

Now we have introduced the concept of community and initially discussed the term community work, and before we move to an outline of the book, it needs noting that the examples given in this work are drawn from British urban community work. Recently there has been a development of texts that examine the increasing and contrasting problems and pressures faced by rural communities in Britain. For example, some sectors of rural areas are experiencing problems of high unemployment, economic instability, depopulation and weakened communities. At the same time other sectors of rural areas are experiencing increasing suburbanization, rising property values and difficulties between the indigenous and newcomers. Recommended texts which examine rural issues are Benfield (1990), Francis and Henderson (1992; 1993), and Henderson and Francis (1992). The case for rural community work is also made by Giarchi (1994).

This book examines the theory and practices of community work in the United Kingdom; however, there are similarities and important contrasting differences with community work practices elsewhere. I hope that readers who are more familiar with community work outside the United Kingdom will find the text helpful, just as British community work has benefited from insights gained abroad.

Outline of the book

In order to explore the theory and practice of contemporary British community work the book follows a particular form which enables this to be undertaken in a systematic and coherent manner.

Chapter 2 explores the development of community work in the United Kingdom from its beginnings at the height of British imperialism, through its re-emergence in the late 1960s, until the present time. This examination reveals distinct elements in its development, originating in particular economic, social and political circumstances. It will be noted that these differing forces, together with developments within the community work movement itself, have, throughout its history, fed into each other. Moving separately and independently, but inevitably linked together, these developments have created what we understand as contemporary community work.

Chapter 3 examines and evaluates the main theories, noted above, that have influenced community work since the 1960s.

Chapter 4 moves the theoretical discussion to consider the significant ideas of the Italian social theorist Antonio Gramsci, who, as we will discover, offers an important interpretation of activities such as community work. Building on this interpretation of community work, the chapter examines and evaluates the role of different types and forms of contemporary social movement which could have implications for a developing understanding of community work theory.

Chapter 5 examines the models which constitute contemporary community work practice. These models have been identified as community care, community organization, community development, social/community planning, community education, and community action. Within community action two further models are located: feminist community work, and black and anti-racist community work.

Chapter 6 examines the practice of community work by identifying five central themes: recruitment; training; employment and funding; skills; and the management of community work.

The final chapter considers the direction community work could take in the future.

Chapter 2

THE DEVELOPMENT OF BRITISH COMMUNITY WORK

Introduction

If we are to examine the contemporary debates within British community work it is important to have a clear understanding of it from its inception at the height of the Empire to the end of the twentieth century. As an enterprise, community work has always been closely influenced by social, political and economic trends (see, for example, Baldock, 1977; Loney, 1983; Waddington, 1983). In this sense the contemporary period is no different from the past. What is important for our discussions is the way in which trends, or features, in community work history have an influence upon, or link into, present-day developments.

British community work emerged from two contradictory and distinct forces: benevolent paternalism as reflected in the work of the Colonial Office and the Settlement Movement; and collective community action such as the Glasgow rent strikes, the unemployed workers' movement, the suffragettes and the colonial struggles for independence. We begin by considering these early forces.

Community work in the colonial tradition

It is difficult to locate a precise date for the commencement of a recognizable form of British community work. However, community development was an integral feature of British imperialism and dates from before the nineteenth century. The discussion surrounding the application by the Colonial Office of community development techniques in Third World countries is well documented (Dominelli, 1990; Halpern, 1963; Kwo, 1984; Marsden and Oakley, 1982; Mayo, 1975). The main purpose of this form of community development was the integration of colonial territories into the capitalist system. The technique involved incorporating the indigenous ruling class into the colonial hegemony by affording them particular status and privileges. In return, support was given to the colonial domination through the collection of taxes and the establishment of a legal system based on that in Britain. One writer claims that while the inhabitants of British colonies may have gained materially and educationally from community development, the context in which this occurred was political: 'gains were made for local people, not by them' (Craig, 1989: 4). Community development was to continue in developing countries after the dismantling of colonialism by playing a key role in combating the spread of communism.

Colonialism in developing countries did not go unchallenged by its populations and there is considerable evidence of rebellions by slaves, and struggles for independence, in countries under British domination (Bolt and Drescher, 1980; Fryer, 1984; Linebaugh, 1982; 1984; Walvin, 1985). The traditions and solidarity established among black people during colonialism, and the resultant anti-colonial struggles, created a black consciousness which was brought to Britain by black settlers and their children (Gilroy, 1987). As we will discuss later, this strengthened and resourced collective action by black people living in Britain, particularly from the early 1950s.

British community work: the early days

Community work within Britain commenced at a later date than its colonial equivalent. Towards the end of the Victorian era British social structure was dominated by two major forces: the ascendancy of the bourgeoisie and the development of the urban working class. The period was marked by the state beginning to take a permanent role in the welfare of its citizens (Thane 1989: vii). Themes of the retreat of the aristocracy and the subsequent ascendancy of the bourgeoisie, the rise of the urban working class and the development of collective responses to education and welfare are closely linked. From the early 1870s the British economy experienced for the first time severe competition from the developing economies in western Europe and the United States. As a consequence the newly established bourgeoisie, which had made its wealth from industry, banking and commerce, became uncertain of its future. Meanwhile members of the new urban working class, which had appeared until then to have passively accepted their subjugated position, were becoming aware of their potential power through the trade union movement and the New Unionism of 1889. The socialist renaissance and the growth of Fabianism from 1884, and of Marxism from 1881, also played a part in raising the consciousness of large numbers of the urban population. The radicalization of the labour movement, the need to secure the support of the new working-class voters (mainly better-off skilled men), together with their own guilt and awareness of the increasing numbers of people in poverty, led the already alarmed bourgeoisie to question the extent to which *laissez-faire* doctrines could effectively deal with persistent and worsening social conditions. The threat to Britain's superior trading position similarly moved the government of the time to examine collectivist solutions to its economic and social dilemmas. In response the Conservative governments of the turn of the century, and the 1906–14 Liberal government, implemented a number of social and educational reforms which were intended to head off class conflict, and to benefit the long-term interests of British capital by equipping its workforce to compete both militarily and economically with its foreign rivals (Gough, 1979: 62). These early collectivist solutions still left room for numerous Victorian charities and self-help groups, including the influential and powerful Charity Organisation Society which was established in 1869.

The Charity Organisation Society was committed to the rational application of charitable assistance to those it considered 'deserving'. In order to separate the 'undeserving' from the 'deserving' poor, families in need were visited by workers who undertook a series of structured and supportive casework visits. This process was the commencement of what was to become known as social work. (For an account of the origins and development of the Charity Organisation Society, see Mowatt, 1961).

One of the founders of the Charity Organisation Society, Canon Samuel Barnett, the vicar of St Jude's in Whitechapel, east London, became increasingly dissatisfied with the organization's inability to address the need to improve the living and working conditions of the poor. Barnett argued that it was necessary for those who gave charity to the poor to live in the areas they served, in order to observe and experience at first hand the problems that arose from poverty. He believed it was possible to establish in poor neighbourhoods settlement houses which offered educational and recreational opportunities for local communities. Following in the wake of the work of an Oxford undergraduate, Arnold Toynbee, and his colleagues, who had spent their summer vacation of 1893 living in Whitechapel in order to study poverty, Barnett formed the University Settlement Association. A year later he established in Commercial Road, East London, the first settlement which he named Toynbee Hall.

Toynbee Hall, which has been described as the 'Mother of Settlements' (Rimmer, 1980), had as its philosophy a belief that if the poor were treated as having the same worth as the rich, class barriers would disappear and material improvement increased. The settlement was designed to accommodate up to 14 university graduates who offered those living in the neighbourhood a range of facilities and educational and recreational classes, including art and music. Toynbee Hall was influential in the early development of community-based intervention in poor areas, and had among its student residents William Beveridge from 1903 to 1907 and Clement Atlee from 1909 to 1910 (Harris, 1977: 43). American students also stayed at Toynbee Hall, and in 1887 they started the College Settlement Association in the United States of America (Rimmer, 1980: 2).

By the end of the nineteenth century 30 settlements based on the model of Toynbee Hall had been established, many in university towns and cities. The settlements were usually residential and university students were able to spend some of their free time living and working in poor neighbourhoods, offering a range of educational classes and welfare services (Thane, 1989: 23). Using his experience of these early settlements, Barnett wrote extensively about the poor, poverty, and the settlement movement (Barnett, 1888; 1904). He outlined in his work his distrust of the cult of the expert, the power of professionalism, and a wish to see social work and community work become less needed and eventually diminished. As indicated, Barnett's views differed from those of the Charity Organisation Society in that he advocated a redistribution of social and economic benefits in favour of the poor, mainly through improvements in health care and education. He also responded to the first volumes of Booth's studies on poverty by questioning whether by themselves the statistics could adequately present the lives of those in poverty. Instead he advocated that the universities should share their cultural riches, arguing that settlements 'intended in the long run to go deeper than philanthropy by making knowledge the common property of all classes' (Parry and Parry, 1979: 25).

We can see that the settlement movement contained within it the beginnings of community work. It was part of a wider response to a range of social, economic and political difficulties facing neighbourhoods in Victorian and Edwardian Britain. Although community work within Britain was not used in the overt manner that it was in the colonies, its purpose was not entirely dissimilar. Instead of the Colonial Office being the main channel for community activity, it was the Anglican Church and the universities. These powerful institutions played a strategic role in the development of community work as a means of both dissolving dissent between the social classes within urban areas, and of addressing the issue of poverty in its broadest sense (Jones, 1976). The community work innovators were upper- and middle-class reformers rather than state functionaries or even political revolutionaries. Many of them in fact reflected the 'reforming evangelical trend in the Church of England' (Parry and Parry, 1979: 24). The settlements were concerned with both the social health of the locality in which they were situated, and in encouraging the development of responsible community leadership. While it can be seen that early settlements were a response to growing social unrest, this form of community work was in essence an example of benevolent paternalism by socially concerned philanthropists. Similarly, under the influence of Barnett's wife, Henrietta, settlements were established replicating the practice of separate university colleges for men and women. It is more accurate to state, however, that there were mixed settlements and women's settlements. In the early days of the settlement movement the men regarded their work in the settlements as a brief interlude before developing a career in another sphere. Women, however, who were faced with career restrictions, saw settlements as offering opportunities for their self-enhancement (Seed, 1973: 29; Walton, 1975: 50). As a result of this the women's settlements linked with the Charity Organisation Society in establishing for the first time professional social work training courses (Parry and Parry, 1979: 25).

We have noted the increasing strength and confidence of the labour movement during the late nineteenth and early twentieth century. In response the state, for reasons discussed above, introduced a number of reforms to advance the well-being of the working class and in turn the profitability of capitalism. The reforms were also aimed at integrating the working class into the values and ideals of the status quo in order to ensure the stability and security of the bourgeoisie. However, resistance to the dominant hegemony was found where class consciousness was strongest and where support could be drawn from 'regional and national loyalties, especially in the Celtic fringe' (Bédarida, 1990: 134). It is not surprising to note, therefore, that one of the earliest recorded forms of community action was in the city of Glasgow. During the early part of the twentieth century there were a number of struggles in Glasgow against the Munitions Act and for the campaign demanding a 40-hour working week. In 1915 both working-class and lower middle-class people demonstrated against increases in rents and the lack of attention to slum housing. Thousands of Glasgow tenants were involved in a rent strike, with protests spreading to other British cities leading to rent strikes and calls for lower rents and improved housing (Damer, 1980). Clydeside employers supported the workers' struggle because the higher rents were creating an unsettled workforce and deterring labour from moving to the area. The outcome was the Rent and Mortgage Interest (Rent Restriction) Act 1915, which restricted rent and mortgage interest rates (Melling, 1980). The victory is considered unique in the history of British community struggles mainly because of the bargaining power of the Glaswegian munitions workers whose labour was crucial during the war effort (Corrigan and Ginsburg, 1975). Working-class collective action was also prevalent in the 1920s and 1930s with the growth of the National Unemployed Workers' Movement (Hannington, 1967; 1977). Craig (1989: 4) believes this development was the first attempt to link struggles in the home with those in the workplace. There is some evidence to support this, although Bagguley (1991: 108) reveals that women were marginalized by the dominance of men in organization of the Movement.

The suffragette movement also played a part in the growth of collective action, although in this case it was almost exclusively bourgeois (Rowbotham 1977; 1992). The direct action and often illegal tactics – including delegations, public demonstrations, and interruption of meetings, and then hunger strikes – were aimed at raising public consciousness for female suffrage. However, it was not until after women had been given new roles in the First World War that they were able to achieve the franchise in 1918. While the 1918 Representation of the People's Act gave the vote for women over 30, it was not until 1928 that women gained voting equality with men. Struggles for these early feminists became known as first-wave feminism. The second wave was not until the late 1960s.

While the economy was in a depressed state during the inter-war period there were a number of innovations within the community work field, including the development by Henry Morris in 1928 of the first Cambridgeshire village college. This innovative, comprehensive community provision marked the commencement nationally of the gradual and often slow development of community schools and colleges (Rée, 1973). Another important innovation that was to have an impact on the growth and direction of community work were community centres. In response to growing unemployment and the public concern for the settling of newcomers to new council estates, the New Estates Community Committee (later titled the Community Centres Association) was founded in 1929 by the British Association of Residential Settlements and the Educational Settlements Association (later titled the British Association of Settlements and Social Action Centres). This committee distributed grants towards the cost of building and maintaining community centres on new estates (Cameron *et al.*, 1943). During the inter-war years the National Council for Social Service also provided £1 million for community centres offering facilities for the unemployed (Marshall, 1975: 81). This gesture was intended in part to counter the alternative facilities offered by the National Unemployed Workers' Movement, whose centres were considered by the National Council for Social Service as potential threats to 'national stability' (Hanson, 1972: 636).

We can see that the development of community work during the economically depressed inter-war years was largely instigated by government-supported agencies, and by the increasingly important settlement movement. These developments were primarily aimed at integrating into broader society those communities suffering from the effects of severe unemployment and undergoing a period of unsettling physical transition. On the political front the era was charged with a great deal of worker unrest which culminated in the General Strike of 1926. According to Beatrice Webb's diaries this was to prove to be 'one of the most significant landmarks in the history of the British working class' (quoted in Cole, 1956: 92). It also signalled a move by the labour movement away from the revolutionary terminology and tactics of the previous forty years to a reformist strategy (Bédarida, 1990: 185). Collective community action of this period was, however, never fully in the revolutionary mode. The ideology of self-help, which was a feature of the Victorian middle class, was also an aspect of working-class life, with the development of the co-operative movement, adult education (the Workers' Educational Association was established in 1903), friendly societies as well as trade unionism reflecting an 'ameliorative rather than revolutionary social philosophy' (Fraser 1984: 108).

Britain in the late 1930s was a divided country. Those in work were enjoying rising real incomes and living standards, while those unemployed were experiencing increasing poverty (Mowatt, 1955; Stevenson and Cook, 1977). It is difficult to trace a history of community work from this period until the end of the Second World War, although we do know that a wide range of voluntary bodies, including the Citizens' Advice Bureaux and the Women's Royal Voluntary Service, were to play a part in the war effort (Calder, 1971).

By the early 1940s the threat of invasion by the Nazis had a major impact upon the British people. After three decades of bitter class confrontation in Britain there was a growing consensus, coupled with a sense of national solidarity, aimed at defeating the common enemy, Adolf Hitler. Writing about the English, one of the leading historians of the time, A.J.P. Taylor, describes this as 'a brief period in which the English people felt they belonged to a truly democratic community' (Taylor, 1965: 550). This experience of solidarity led Richard Titmus to comment that there was after the war a new attitude towards social policy, with general agreement and a willingness 'to accept a great increasing of egalitarian policies and collective state intervention' (quoted in Harris, 1981: 43). This was to lead to the post-war social-democratic consensus and an organized welfare state.

Community work in social democracy

The early post-war years were a period of social reform premised on a harmony of interests between capital and labour. This agreement became known as the social-democratic consensus. It was built on the labour movement's acceptance that the advantages of capital could be delivered to working people. In return the ruling class accepted that it could, and should, provide improvements to working-class life and conditions. This is a central concept in the developing relationship between the state and community work which we will examine in more detail in Chapter 3.

The British public's wish to see a political consensus was demonstrated in the overwhelming victory of the Labour Party in the 1945 general election. The Labour Party, with a manifesto arguing for higher and more proportional direct taxation in return for greater state provision, gained a substantial, 146-seat majority with 47.8% of the votes cast (Butler and Sloman, 1976). This gave Labour a mandate to carry out sweeping economic changes, structural social reforms and the introduction of the modern welfare state.

The social-democratic consensus was built upon an expanding and confident national and international economy. The British economy prospered from a long economic boom, which stretched from the mid-1940s until the early 1970s, reflected in rising levels of output and living standards, low unemployment, and expanded trade (Harris, 1988: 14). During the 1950s the Conservative Party enjoyed popularity at the polls and the Labour Party, after its brief but important period in office, consolidated itself as an effective party in opposition. It appeared to be a time of affluence, with the development of consumer markets for cars, washing machines and longer holidays. It was also a period when a complacent air of the affluent society pervaded institutions, while conventional wisdom held that the economy was benefiting everyone. This was further reflected and encouraged by government ministers (Bogdanor and Skidelsky, 1970; Sked and Cook, 1984). Meanwhile community work played a part in the development of the social-democratic consensus with the continuing activity through local councils of social services and the community centres in new housing estates. Thus, the dominant mode of community work was largely within the voluntary sector (Thomas, 1983: 18).

The dominant complacent view that the British economy was delivering the affluent society to all its citizens was being challenged by the late 1950s.

One challenge came from the growth of sociology and social policy as critical subjects and led, in part, to the rediscovery in the 1960s of poverty (Abel-Smith and Townsend, 1965; Coates and Silburn, 1970; Hobsbawm, 1968). At the same time a number of community studies were being carried out that revealed the decline of traditional (and often idealized) working-class spirit, and working-class communities, and the breakdown of social control (Frankenberg, 1969; Loudon, 1961; Wilmott, 1963). At grassroots level there were examples of community action, most notably in the form of squatting in government-owned premises, because of the shortage of adequate housing provision by the state (Craig, 1989: 6).

From the early 1950s community work theory, which was beginning to be developed in North America, began to have an impact upon theory and practice in Britain. Perhaps the most influential community work book of the time was written by a Canadian, Murray Ross (1955). It has been suggested that his work 'captured the imagination of staff in councils of social service because it suggested there was a theoretical basis for their work, and set about community work as neighbourhood work . . . and . . . as interagency work' (Smith 1979: 65). So an interesting phenomenon was taking place. While community work practice was developing in Britain, it was in North America that community work theory began to emerge. These early texts were then used by British community workers. The first British attempts to construct a distinct theory of community work can be seen in the work of Batten, who had been engaged in community development in Nigeria from 1927 to 1949. Batten was critical of the use of community development as a means to perpetuate colonial domination (Batten, 1967: v). During this time he became associated with the non-directive approach to community development which, as we will note in Chapter 3, was to influence early community work training (Batten, 1957; 1962; 1965).

In Britain the influential report by Younghusband (1959) identified community work as a third method of social work intervention alongside case work and group work. The work by Kuenstler (1961) was to develop this concept, and by the beginning of the 1960s there were a number of workers who described themselves as 'community workers', and the term 'community work' was in general use (Jones, 1983: 1). By the middle of the decade community work was 'tied intellectually to social work' (Thomas, 1983: 21), although there was little evidence of community work practice within social services departments.

The development of British community work was gathering pace when the Calouste Gulbenkian Foundation was approached by workers to sponsor a conference and an enquiry into the activity. The Gulbenkian Foundation agreed to this request and published a significant report which was to promote and debate the nature and purpose of community work, while exploring the role of community workers and the issues they confronted (Calouste Gulbenkian Foundation, 1968). Jones (1983: 2) believes the lack of attention in the report to the conflictual relationship between community work and political activity did not reflect the extensive discussions within the working party, which was drawn from practitioners. One can only speculate as to the reasons for this. Perhaps one reason for the final consensus was the influence of its chairperson, Dame Eileen Younghusband, who perceived community work as a new form of social work (Thomas, 1983: 30). Another reason may have been the power of the prestigious and wealthy Gulbenkian Foundation which funded the report. What is known is that the report of the Seebohm Committee (HMSO, 1968) was to be of greater significance in the development of the activity by confirming the adoption of community work methods by social work and in helping to create the occupation of community work.

The 'golden age' of British community work

If there was a 'golden age' of community work it was the period from 1968 until the mid- to late 1970s. It was a time when community work grew as an activity in both statutory and voluntary sectors, as the state became increasingly involved in the task of addressing social, political and economic change. This section begins by considering the national and international events that created a sense of change in the late 1960s. It continues by exploring two major influences on community work during this period: the Urban Programme and the Community Development Projects. It then considers other important contemporary themes, including: extra-parliamentary activities; the work of the Gulbenkian Foundation; the influence of the women's movement; the concern with racial unrest; plans for inner-city areas; the role of the Manpower Services Commission; and the continuing decline in the British economy and the resultant industrial and political changes.

The wider context

The year 1968 proved to be a watershed in world-wide developments as well as a landmark in the evolution of community work. In the wider context, 1968 was a year of revolt, rebellion and reaction throughout the world, with a catalogue of events which included: the student and worker struggles in Paris during May; student demonstrations and occupations at universities in several countries, including Britain; the Vietnamese Tet Offensive against American imperialism; world-wide protest and demonstrations against US involvement in Vietnam; racial riots in the United States; the assassinations of Martin Luther King and Robert Kennedy; the US Civil Right's Bill; the invasion and occupation of Czechoslovakia by Warsaw Pact troops; civil rights activists in Derry defying the government's ban on their marching; and the first mass open-air rock concert in Britain. It was a year of turmoil and change and, to quote one commentator, 'a year after which nothing could ever be the same again, a year which divides epochs, and a year which branded a generation for life' (Kettle, 1988: 3).

By the late 1960s the British economy was experiencing a deepening economic crisis, with the worsening of unemployment, and the devaluation of sterling which led the government to deploy new forms of social intervention in those areas thought to be worse effected by the country's changing fortunes. The state, aware of the need to respond to the growing economic and social changes, commissioned a number of reports which recognized the failure of the welfare state to meet the needs of disadvantaged and marginal groups, and of capital's need for a stable, well-integrated workforce. These reports advocated further intervention in working-class areas and assisted in the increased profile of community work. The most significant of these reports were: the Ingleby Report (Home Office, 1960), which, published earlier in the decade, recognized the role of family advice centres and the need to undertake preventive social work with children and young people, and led to the establishment of neighbourhood and family centres; the Skeffington Report (HMSO, 1969), which recommended increased, if limited, public participation in planning; the Plowden Report (DES, 1967), which advocated a significant programme of positive discrimination in the primary education sector, including the development of local projects aimed at strengthening the relationship between the home, school and community; and the Fairbairn-Milson Report (DES, 1969), which urged youth work to develop a community perspective.

Two major innovations of long-term significance in the development of British community work that evolved at the same time were the Urban Programme, established in 1968, and the Community Development Projects, launched in 1969 as an element of the Urban Programme.

The Urban Programme

The Urban Programme emerged as a response by the Labour government to Enoch Powell's 'Rivers of Blood' speech, which predicted racial tension in British cities similar to that witnessed in the United States (Powell, 1968: 99), and the government's concern to be seen to be acting on rising public panic to immigration and race relations (Foot, 1969: 112). With unemployment increasing from the early 1960s, both the Conservative and Labour governments had begun restricting immigration from the developing world while at the same time attempting to enhance the integration of those immigrants already settled. The 1962 and 1968 Commonwealth Immigrants Acts restricted immigration, while the 1965 and 1968 Race Relations Acts took the first steps towards outlawing discrimination and establishing the Community Relations Commission. The government was in effect signalling a mixed message. On the one hand it was claiming that black people were a 'problem' by restricting entry, while on the other hand it was advocating that the white indigenous population should welcome the new settlers. The Urban Programme was, therefore, part of a policy of containing the 'problem' of black people living in urban areas. It was not a coincidence that at central government level race relations and the new Urban Programme were the responsibility of the same parliamentary under-secretary (Edwards and Batley, 1978: 38–9). The development of the Urban Programme was preceded by Section 11 of the Local Government Act of 1966 which provided 75% central government funding to specific projects in areas where 2% or more of the population were from the New Commonwealth.

The Urban Programme was not restricted to 'black areas' partly 'for fear of provoking accusations of favoured treatment for immigrants' (Loney, 1983: 34), and it proved ineffective at reaching ethnic minority groups (Demuth, 1977). In practice, many local authorities and voluntary organizations in different parts of Britain applied through the Urban Programme for aid to combat local pockets of deprivation, defined in terms of social indicators: unemployment, overcrowding, large families, poor environment, immigrant concentrations, and children in care or in need of care. The social indicators were never quantified and aid was allocated on a 75:25 basis by central and local government. In concert with the social-democratic consensus of targeting the funds to 'areas of deprivation' the state allowed no recognition for the 'widespread consequences of economic and industrial decline as they affected the working class in general' (Bolger *et al.*, 1981: 122). From the Urban Programme, the Inner Area Programme evolved and included the Inner Area Partnership Schemes and the Free Enterprise Zones. In 1975 responsibility for the Urban Programme was transferred from the Home Office to the Department of Environment (Laurence and Hall, 1981: 93), and after the introduction of the Inner Urban Areas Act 1978, the Urban Programme was recast 'in more of an economic development than social welfare mould' (Boddy, 1984: 162), reflecting increasing recognition during the late 1970s of the need economically to regenerate the inner cities, often with private rather than public capital.

Through these various Urban Programme initiatives millions of pounds were distributed to a plethora of community work projects. In 1987 it was supporting approximately 4,000 voluntary and community work projects (Taylor and Presley, 1987) although by the mid-1980s overall Urban Programme resources were declining in real terms (Whitting *et al.*, 1986). The reasons for the longevity of the Urban Programme are various. One of the most succinct explanations is as follows:

Despite (or perhaps because of) continual review and sometimes long periods of uncertainty, the Urban Programme has survived, it has attracted ministerial attention and interest and has involved a continuing central/local partnership at a time when central/local relations have been at their lowest ebb. In part this robustness has stemmed from bipartisan recognition of the problems of inner areas as well as from the consensus between central and local government that economic regeneration of inner areas was a priority.

(Whitting *et al.*, 1986: 15)

However, the relatively small sums of finance allocated to the Urban Programme were 'dwarfed' by financial cuts applied to inner-city local authorities (Benyon and Solomos, 1987: 193). On a more specific level, one reason for the Urban Programme's long life could reside in that part of the programme that was concerned with targeting relatively small amounts of money for important but politically 'safe' activities and projects which receive warm appeal in the communities in which they are located. Provision for children and community projects are two areas that have attracted regular funding over the years (Laurence and Hall, 1981: 92–3). The Urban Programme was also used by the government during the 1980s to employ workers with the young unemployed and to support financially projects such as those targeted at young black offenders, community-based projects catering for 16–21-year-old unemployed people, and neighbourhood projects involved in a range of activities including youth work, play schemes and clubs for older people. Overall, it can be noted that the Urban Programme greatly assisted the occupation of community work to grow and diversify and to stimulate the development of the activity in both the voluntary and statutory sectors. However, the pervasive feature of the various schemes was their use of short-term funding which did little to counter the reputation of community work as being experimental and tokenistic.

The Community Development Projects

The other major development of state-supported community work during the late 1960s were the Community Development Projects. These developed from the social-democratic consensus philosophy which argued that a minority of the population were victims of a range of related problems. When initiated, the projects supported a community pathology model of poverty that argued that people in disadvantaged communities failed to compete in the marketplace because of internal community or personal problems rather than structural inequalities. The projects were to assist people to use the social services more constructively and to reduce dependence on these services by stimulating community change (Mayo, 1980). However, the workers and researchers employed on the Community Development Projects, which were located in 12 'deprived areas' (Batley, Canning Town, Cumbria, Coventry, Glyncorrwg, Liverpool, Newcastle upon Tyne, North Shields, Oldham, Southwark and Paisley), rejected the Conservative explanations of poverty and inner-city deprivation, many of which were articulated by the late Lord Joseph who was aligned to the 'cycle of deprivation' view of poverty in society (Joseph, 1972). Instead, the staff produced a radical critique that demonstrated the structural basis of poverty which was perpetuated by social structures, and which created an unequal distribution of resources and power throughout society. The poor inhabiting the 'deprived areas' were therefore identified as essential for the continuance of capitalism. (Unfortunately space does not allow me to discuss the examples of the locally based Community Developments Projects. Appendix A provides a select bibliography of Community Development Project reports and publications.) Successive governments did not take kindly to the project teams' analysis and by 1976 the state had withdrawn its funding to what it had originally conceived as an experiment in the co-ordination of central and local government and voluntary sector resources (Green, 1992). The central state was not the only critic of the Community Development Projects; there is evidence that the team's Marxist analysis was also criticized by local authorities and communities for its radical perspective (McKay and Cox, 1979). However, the point should not be lost that the Community Development Projects' analysis (that structural inequalities were the root cause of poverty and an integral aspect of capitalism), was the central reason for the state's swift action to silence the radicals (Loney, 1983). As we will discuss in Chapter 3, the Community Development Projects, which were the largest and most controversial of all the government-sponsored community work programmes, were also the clearest example of the radical and socialist approach to community work theory and practice.

Further significant developments

By the end of the 1960s there were a number of strands feeding into the development of community work. We have noted the impact of national and international world events which were to assist in the creation, particularly among young people, of a counter-culture and a new thinking and understanding of a challenge to the political, social and economic affairs of the period. The Labour Party in office was to disappoint the social reformers who were hoping for a transformation in society and a move to a greater redistribution of Britain's wealth and income. The rise and decline of the Campaign for Nuclear Disarmament as a vehicle for protest against the government, and the development of single-issue pressure groups such as Shelter and the Child Poverty Action Group – which was set up at Toynbee Hall in 1965 (Briggs and Macartney, 1984) – as a result of the rediscovery of poverty, were symptomatic of extra-parliamentary activities. These pressure groups were formed as a challenge to and in response to the disillusionment with conventional politics. These, together with the growing number of critical intellectuals in the social sciences, the radical ideas and literature of the New Left, the decline of Britain's economic performance, the increasing concern in government circles that the welfare state was failing to integrate certain individuals and communities, and the fear of urban unrest focused primarily around the issue of immigration, led in different ways to an increase and expansion in locally based community work projects. As we have noted, the majority of these projects were government initiated and funded by the government, with community work being one of a number of interventions aimed in part at diffusing possible radical protest and managing economic and social change. There was, however, a profusion of locally initiated community action projects that centred around development concerns and rent increases. Similarly, the government-funded community programmes were, as we have seen in the example of the Community Development Projects, staffed by workers influenced by a political analysis that was critical of the structural inequalities within a capitalist society. However, as Waddington (1983: 42) recalls, the analysis of the majority of community workers 'basically reflected a gut reaction against bureaucracy and a rather unspecific idealism which owed rather more to the ideals of the "alternative society" than to the thinking of the New Left'.

Among other significant features of community work's evolution was the establishment of the Association of Community Workers, and the launching of the *Community Development Journal* by Oxford University Press, both of which are still in existence. Although there are no data to provide a reliable indicator of the growth of community work during this period, it is agreed that by the early 1970s community work was rapidly developing and, to quote Waddington (1983: 42) further, was feeding off

> the annual surplus of a growing economy and was part of a system of public sector redistribution to disadvantaged and marginal groups, a form of 'kitty bargaining' which helped to give substance to the claims of pluralist politics. The progressive adoption of community work by the state has – amongst other reasons – followed recognition of its value as a tool to reinforce a flagging belief in social democracy, especially amongst economically marginal groups.

During the 1970s the state continued to be the prime funder of community work both through the public sector and in its grant aid to the voluntary sector. One of the most significant grant-making trusts outside the state was the Calouste Gulbenkian Foundation, which between 1970 and 1979 granted nearly £2 million to community work and community relations. Much of the work funded was experimental and innovatory, while the Foundation was to play a significant role in raising the profile of community work through its many publications, training events, conferences and national networking. The Foundation was able to claim that it had a role in government policy-making in relation to community work and in the establishment of the Federation of Community Work Groups (Mills, 1983: 86). The Foundation also appointed Lord Boyle to chair what became known as the Community Work Group, which brought together senior representatives from a range of statutory bodies and voluntary organizations engaged in the development of community work.

The increasing significance of gender and race

The women's liberation movement re-emerged in Britain during the early 1970s after 'the stirrings of consciousness in the late 1960s' (Rowbotham, 1989: xii) and the first women's liberation conference of 1970. During the 1970s the women's movement and society's increased awareness of women's position were to play a crucial part in the development of community work. On closer examination we can see that there were three main factors in the development of feminist community work. One was the significant role women played (and continue to play) in the communities or neighbourhoods in which they reside. In our society women are charged with the main responsibility of childrearing and are therefore more likely to spend longer periods in their homes and communities than men. Consequently, issues related to their living accommodation, and to the health and welfare of their children and themselves, are closer to their experience than to men's (Curno *et al.*, 1982; Mayo, 1977). Secondly, during the 1970s social inequality of women became a public issue. This was due in part to the increased voice of the emerging women's liberation movement; to the developing under-standing by many women, and in some cases men, that women's position was subordinate to that of men's; and to the recognition by the state of women's situation. For instance, in 1975 the Equal Pay Act (passed in 1970), came into force, the Sex Discrimination Act was passed and the Equal Op-portunities Commission established. Thirdly, during the 1960s and early 1970s community work theory and practice was an activity dominated by white males. The Community Development Projects which were leading the development of radical community work were similarly gender-blind. Although the Community Development Projects were working to alleviate poverty they failed to recognize and appreciate the particular concerns of women in poverty (Dominelli, 1990; Green and Chapman, 1990). However, as the decade progressed the number of campaigns and organizations initi-ated and run by women increased. The number of female community work-ers grew, together with the emergence of the community work literature written by women, and since the 1970s feminist theory has made a significant impact on community work which we will address further in Chapter 3.

We have noted that a strong push for the establishment of the Urban Programme came from a fear of unrest around the issue of 'race' which was, and still is, a centrally important issue within British society. This was also a factor in the development during the 1960s of the national Community Relations Commission and the Race Relations Board (which were subsumed by the Commission for Racial Equality in 1976), and local Community Rela-tions Councils (now usually termed Racial Equality Councils) which have displayed a variety of community work styles (Barker, 1981). During this period both the Commission for Racial Equality, by funding community work projects and research, and the local Community Relations Councils in their initiation of grassroots work, were involved in combating discrimin-atory treatment of black people and in supporting community groups and organizations.

State co-option of community work

During the 1970s, the state continued with its drive to improve the inner areas of cities and developed a range of strategies which were aimed at upgrading the physical environment while meeting the needs of people living in certain specified areas. All the above in different ways were to con-tribute to the development of community work. For instance, the experi-mental Comprehensive Community Programme, launched in 1974 and aimed at analysing and meeting the needs of areas of deprivation, and the Inner Area Studies carried out by consultants between 1972 and 1977 (which ad-vocated a 'total approach' to an understanding of urban problems), both had as part of their brief an involvement in community issues. Both experiments adopted the social planning approach, the main elements of which are inter-agency work, and project and service development. The development of the social planning approach within community work was from this period onwards advocated by Thomas (1978), who saw a link between community work, policy development and corporate planning. The government initiative which was to reshape the physical environment of many urban neighbourhoods was the 1974 Housing Act which introduced Housing Action Areas and was intended to rehabilitate specified 'deprived areas'. An effect of this legislation was to take the sting out of 'stop the bulldozer' campaigns, with the possibilities of community workers bringing together local authority departments to plan Housing Action Areas on the basis of need, rather than political expediency (Twelvetrees, 1983: 31).

With an increase in state-sponsored community work in the 1970s it was perhaps inevitable that many community workers would find themselves in potential and actual conflict with their employers, who were also the providers of the services community groups were criticizing. These dilemmas are discussed in some detail by Cockburn (1977) and the London Edinburgh Weekend Return Group (1980). The first half of the 1970s was similar to the late 1960s in that a strong theme within community work was its dual role as part of the welfare state while at the same time being critical of the state's inability to reach some of the poorest sections of society. Community work was also critical of the inferior level of public services being offered to the less well off – a matter of poor services for poor people. The guiding premise for many community workers of the period was empowerment, justice and equality. Yet for all the statements of the Labour governments of 1964–70 and 1974–9 committing them to ameliorating poverty and to opening up society to greater equality, little was achieved in this direction, which led community workers to experience government as unresponsive and uncaring towards the needs of millions of poor people.

The recession of the mid-1970s

By the mid-1970s Britain, along with other countries, began to experience an economic recession, due mainly to the aftermath of the Arab–Israeli war of October 1973 which led Arab oil producers to reduce their supplies and increase the price of exported oil. Within a few months Britain's oil import bill had quadrupled, which considerably weakened its already poor trade balance. The problem was further compounded by the deliberate drive during the previous years to increase Britain's dependence on oil at the expense of home-produced coal. The decision of the National Union of Mineworkers (NUM) to implement a ban on overtime and weekend working from November 1973, in support of a pay claim in excess of the Conservative government's income policy, led to the declaration of a State of Emergency. The government and trade union movement eventually exhausted all negotiating procedures. The NUM called a national miners' strike, while the government announced a general election for February 1974. This was not before: public sector cuts of £1.2 million; a rise in the bank minimum lending rate from $11^{1}/_{4}$% to 13%; a three-day working week for most industrial workers; the disruption (including the use of mass picketing) of coal deliveries to power stations; and 'a scene of industrial bitterness perhaps unparalleled since the General Strike of 1926' (Sked and Cook, 1984: 290). These extra-ordinary events were to herald the beginnings of a decline in the post-war social-democratic consensus and to create the foundations for the rise of the New Right within the Conservative Party which, under the leadership of Margaret Thatcher, was to gain political power five years later.

The incoming minority Labour government of February 1974 quickly re-solved the three-day week and miners' strike and in the following October won a further general election with an increased majority. However, by 1975 the government was presiding over the largest recorded balance-of-payments deficit, unemployment at 700,000 (which would rise to 1.2 million by the following year and to nearly 1.5 million in 1977), and inflation at over 24%. In response, a further £900 million was cut from the public sector, followed by more planned cuts for 1977–78. These measures failed to stem the dra-matic slide in the value of sterling and the government was forced to secure a loan from the International Monetary Fund in exchange for increases in taxation and further cuts in public expenditure amounting to £3,000 million over the following two years.

The economic crisis of the 1960s was, then, relatively minor compared with the problems facing Britain in the mid-1970s which were to have a marked impact on the development of community work. The most signifi-cant feature within community work was the move community workers, together with many other state employees, made from attacking the welfare state to one of defensive struggle. The anti-statism inherent in the philo-sophy and practice of many community workers was, according to Lees and Mayo (1984: 31), to prove inadequate as a 'basis from which to grapple with the challenge from the anti-statism of monetarists'. Community work became one of the constituents of the welfare state that lost out in the rea-ligned social work and education departments, which were competing for declining real resources. From this period onwards the overriding concern of these departments was to provide statutory or mandatory services. If there was any remaining finance it was used for non-statutory programmes which could include community work. Similarly, voluntary organizations that depended upon state support began to experience greater scrutiny of their work and reductions in their funding. Community workers were in some disarray because the emphasis of the state was to finance and support the making of profits in the private sector at the expense of investment in the public sector. This change was to highlight a contradiction within community work which has been well described by Waddington (1983), who argues that social reform had provided the 'baits' which stimulated community work during the 1960s and 1970s. He argued that the removal of these 'baits' was

> a major cause of the falling off of levels of community action and the disorientation of community workers. The plain fact is that many com-munity work activities, as we originally conceived them, have simply lost their point. Our current predicament is that we are no longer col-lectively quite sure of what we are trying to do or how to do it.
>
> (Waddington, 1983: 43)

Perhaps one of the clearest examples of the dilemmas facing community workers during the 1970s recession was the use of Manpower Services Commission schemes to fund the practice. Launched in January 1974 as a means of centralizing responses to growing unemployment, the Manpower Services Commission continually sought methods of reducing the number of people on the unemployment register created by the effects of deindustrialization, while providing low-cost employment and training opportunities for young people and adults. The outcome was a number of schemes, some of which were based in community work projects. The Community Programme, for instance, provided part-time temporary jobs in community settings for the long-term unemployed. The majority of Community Programme workers were male, with more than 65% aged under 25 and most graduates of other unemployment schemes (Finn, 1987: 189). This raised among community work practitioners, a dilemma they were unable satisfactorily to resolve. One group of community workers argued that the activity should have nothing to do with temporary employment schemes which exploited its participants and which could reduce the opportunities for radical change. The opposing argument accepted the thrust of this position but claimed that local communities needed the resources, the employment and the training offered by the Manpower Services Commission. The key, they argued, was to understand this paradox and secure the best deal possible in the interests of local communities (Ellison, 1988; Jones, 1986). By the mid-1980s it was estimated that the Manpower Services Commission was the major funder of community work in Britain, but mainstream community workers vigorously pointed out that the meaning of 'community work' as envisaged by the Commission was at variance with that given to it by the activity itself (Hill, 1987; Craig, 1989).

It appeared that by the close of the decade the golden age of community work had disappeared. Its swift development through the late 1960s and during the early 1970s was halted by the increasing reductions in public expenditure together with a changing philosophy within society which was emphasizing the need for people to 'stand on their own two feet'. The ascending political creed emphasized self-help and voluntary effort, with projects encouraged to look to the private sector for support and finance.

The New Right and community work

In 1979 the Conservative Party under the leadership of Margaret Thatcher won the general election, made a break with the social-democratic consensus and in its place installed a particular form of potentially authoritarian domination which, according to Hall (1988), threatened to discipline Britain for its own ends. The manifesto on which the Conservatives won the election reflected the thinking and the influence of the New Right whose advocates included the US economist and Nobel Prize winner, Professor Milton Friedman, another Nobel laureate in economics, Professor Friedrich von Hayek, and right-wing 'think tanks' including the Institute of Economic Affairs, the Social

Affairs Unit, the Centre for Policy Studies, and the Adam Smith Institute. During the election campaign the Conservatives exploited the popular discontent with the post-war consensus for welfare, health, education and housing, and promised to reverse the relative decline in the British economy and in the values which they argued were affecting Britain's ability to address its future destination. To quote Thatcher reflecting on this time:

> I believe that five years ago the British people made me Prime Minister primarily because they sensed that socialism had been leading them a life of debilitating dependency on the state, when what they really wanted was the independence and freedom of self-reliance and responsibility.
>
> (*Financial Times*, 24 July 1986)

The key principles enshrined in what became known as Thatcherism were the primacy of wealth creation; the regulation of distribution through market principles, accompanied by the notion of individual rather than public choice; redistribution based upon the 'trickle-down' theory; an attack on, and a restructuring of, the state's welfare responsibilities; the comprehensive deregulation of large areas of public and private activity; an assault on the influence of the trade union movement; and the notion of absolute poverty as opposed to relative poverty.

Although the Thatcher government was hostile to the welfare state and collectivism, the first years of its period in office were spent changing the priorities and the emphases rather than mounting an overt attack on the post-war creation. For instance, the government introduced measures to encourage the growth of private health insurance, private hospitals and health care, assisted places in private schools and, through the Housing Act of 1980, the sale of council houses to tenants. There were, however, severe reductions in housing: public sector completions dropped from 104,000 in 1979 to 49,200 in 1982, the lowest figure since the 1920s (Sked and Cook, 1984: 349). According to Walker (1987: 1) what was beginning on a broader scale was the government's 'indifference and, in some instances, outright antagonism towards poor families and the social services on which they depend'.

This indifference and antagonism was believed to be a feature of the Thatcher government's attitude towards the poor and the welfare state, and was evidenced by the increasing poverty and unemployment; by an increasing divide between the rich and the poor and between those living in the 'North' and the 'South'; by a growth in the impoverishment of women and black people; and by encouraging growth in the stigmatization and marginalization of claimants. It was argued that the creation of this more sharply divided society was an essential component of the social and economic policies pursued by the government in its desire to institute a 'sound economy based on free enterprise and individual family responsibility' (Walker, 1987: 1).

The rise of the New Right was accompanied by an economic recession which was borne disproportionately by the poor. For instance, between 1979 and 1986 female unemployment rose by 189% and male unemployment by

143% (Equal Opportunities Commission, 1986). Within these figures there is clear evidence that women and black people were adversely affected (Williams, 1989). In 1985 nearly 30% of the population were living in or on the margins of poverty (140% of Supplementary Benefit level or below) compared with 22% of the population in 1979 (CPAG, 1988); 141,860 'households' were accepted as homeless by local authorities in 1992 (Hutson and Liddiard, 1994); over 11,000 'households' were living in bed and breakfast accommodation in the same year (Burrows and Walentowicz, 1992); and in 1985 the children of unskilled workers were more than twice as likely to die before their first birthday as those born to professional workers (HMSO, 1988).

Advocates of the New Right were to find that their theory did not produce the results they expected and resulted in a continuation of Britain's economic decline. One commentator described this in the following way:

> Public expenditure and taxation has been restructured but not reduced. A very large income transfer towards the upper income groups has been engineered with a corresponding significant increase in poverty. There has been an enormous shake-out of labour but few signs of the permanent increase in productivity needed to improve competitiveness.
>
> (Gamble, 1988: 199)

The Conservative government did not perform the promised economic miracle. In fact the gross national product of Britain grew less during the Thatcher period than in the 1950s, 1960s and 1970s, and Britain became the first industrial nation to import more manufactured goods than it exported (Coutts and Godley, 1989; Johnson, 1991). However, New Right thinking had a significant impact upon the welfare state during the 1980s and in turn had implications for the development of community work.

Despite the influence of New Right thinking in the Thatcher government, community work enjoyed an expansion during the 1980s. A survey undertaken in 1983 of community workers in the United Kingdom indicated that 5,000 practitioners were employed at the time, compared with little more than 1,000 in the early 1970s (Francis et al., 1984). One writer believes this increase was due to: many agencies redesignating jobs and adding the term 'community' to their titles; the state's policy of community care and the resultant 'layer of workers, albeit low-paid, to implement its strategy of shifting the burden of welfare work from public collective to private individual shoulders' (Craig, 1989: 12); and to the growth in the number of workers required to operate a battery of Manpower Services Commission employment schemes. The 1980s were distinguishable by the government's push to encourage the development of strategies in the community for the care of older people and people with disabilities while cutting expenditure on health and social services (DHSS, 1989; Wagner, 1988). A central aspect of New Right philosophy was the need for welfare services to demonstrate increased efficiency and effectiveness before being allocated further public funds. Meanwhile the state encouraged the voluntary and private sectors to fill the vacuum (Iliffe, 1985). It was in this changed context that community work found itself being employed. During the 1980s a philosophy and practice of community social work evolved within social work which drew from pluralist community work ideas of working in small areas called 'patches', and from the skills acquired through working with informal networks (Barclay, 1982; Hadley et al., 1987). Established in a number of local authorities, social work teams employed the community social work approach while setting up 'self-help' groups and organizations, community care schemes, and by encouraging a range of voluntary organizations, including the settlements, to provide a social work service at a reduced cost per client. Community work in this context became used by local authorities to discharge its responsibilities for caring for its citizens within a budget limited by central government. In the process of encouraging community work the state ensured that the activity's boundaries were closely drawn in an attempt to avoid the experiences it had encountered during the 1970s when the Community Development Projects criticized the state for its role in supporting the excesses of capitalism.

Meanwhile, during the 1980s community work, in its more traditional role, was frequently used by the state as a means of intervening at the neighbourhood level to dampen social and political unrest. The violent disorder in a number of British urban areas during 1980, 1981, 1985 and 1986 was thought by a number of writers, including Benyon and Solomos (1987), to have its roots in unemployment, deprivation, racism, political exclusion and police malpractices. The feeling of many young people living in disadvantaged circumstances was that government programmes were failing to meet their needs and they therefore felt they had little stake in society or its institutions (Benyon and Solomos, 1987: 184). At the time of the disorders the government appointed a Cabinet committee to examine inner-city policy and the Urban Programme, so offering the overall appearance that it was dealing with the issues raised by them. The government also appointed a 'Minister for Merseyside', Michael Heseltine, the Environment Secretary, who was given the task of regenerating one of the areas, Toxteth in Liverpool, that had experienced rioting. Little else was undertaken by the state other than a public inquiry into the riots in Brixton, south London, which produced the Scarman Report (HMSO, 1981). This report made a number of recommendations in relation to the role and training of the police, who in response developed more effective means of handling future disorders. Throughout this period the Urban Programme and the Inner City Partnership schemes were used to fund local community projects in areas that experienced unrest. Community work was again employed as a palliative when the substantial resources needed to overcome the major injustices were not forthcoming.

The Manpower Services Commission continued to be a major funder of community work during the decade, with Smith (1989) providing evidence that it was spending over £8 million on community projects in Sheffield, while the local authority spent only £1.5 million on community work. As the main funder of welfare workers in the city, the Commission issued an instruction to workers to refrain from engaging in welfare rights campaign work. This control of community work to ensure projects' 'political neutrality' was registered by a range of community workers dependent on state funding.

Similarly, reductions in local and central government budgets led to a decline in many local community resource centres which were often pivotal in community struggles on housing, health and women's issues (*Community Action*, 83, Spring 1990).

Community work in the 1990s: the changing world

In the spring of 1990 the final issue of *Community Action* was published. This national magazine, a brightly burning beacon in the community work field for almost 20 years, finally succumbed to the exhaustion of its voluntary workers and a decline in resources for radical community work. The magazine was absorbed into *Public Service Action*, published by Services to Community Action and Tenants. The closure of this independent, non-profit-making magazine was a significant and symbolic event in the community work field and reflected the changing world community work was now moving into.

Responsibility for the various programmes for the unemployed, Employment Training and Youth Training, were devolved by the government in the early 1990s from its own agency (successively the Manpower Services Commission, the Training Commission, the Training Agency and the Employment Service) to 82 regional Training and Enterprise Councils in England and Wales and 22 Local Enterprise Councils in Scotland. These councils, which are presently managed by directors of large private firms, with only a minor involvement by educationalists, unions and local authorities, are part of a drive to encourage employers to take further financial and practical responsibility for training future workers. The Community Programme, which was an important source of funding for different forms of community work, has disappeared. In its place the government introduced a 'Community Action Programme', intended to provide 60,000 part-time 'community work places' for those people unemployed for more than a year (Weston, 1993).

The Urban Programme, which has historically been a linchpin in the development of community work, is under threat in the 1990s. In place of the Urban Programme, the government has revealed new proposals which are discussed in more detail in the section on community work employment and funding in Chapter 6.

The community charge (widely known as the poll tax), which was introduced in Scotland in April 1989, and in England and Wales a year later, proved to be one of the most unpopular taxes of modern times. The flat-rate local tax led to wealthy and poor people alike receiving similar tax demands. In response, one of the largest mass movements in British history, which at its peak involved over 17 million people (Burns, 1992), formed to demonstrate and protest against what was considered to be a major injustice. The effects of the tax were far-reaching, with many people having

to pay bills which were two or three times higher than before. This was because the costs of administration were twice as high and because dramatic reductions in the tax bills of the wealthy were paid for by ordinary people.

(Burns, 1992: 10)

Local authorities came under increasing financial pressure as large numbers of people withheld all or part of their tax, and those councils that budgeted for more expenditure than central government permitted, faced rate-capping. In an attempt to keep within budgets, local authorities reduced a number of their services, including resources for community work (Taylor, 1992: 15).

The changes local authorities underwent in the 1980s continued in the 1990s, and it has been argued that local government is being transformed to fit into a new business-led provider of welfare (Butcher *et al.*, 1990; Cochrane, 1993). The developments in care in the community following the 1990 National Health Service and Community Care Act reflected this trend and, according to one observer, offer us 'a striking Thatcherite synthesis of the free market' (Langan, 1990: 59). The role taken by local authorities since April 1993, when community care legislation came into force, is that of ser- vice enabler. With new funding arrangements local authorities now contract in various welfare functions and services, with community organizations and groups, along with private care agencies, competing to provide them. This ideological and practical shift is thought by some to assist in redressing the balance between professionals and the public, with Taylor (1992: 20) arguing that community development has 'an important role in making this work'. The concern must be that community work could be used to offer low-cost strategies to tackle problems that demand substantial resources.

On a wider front, the Council of Europe (1989) endorsed the importance of community development, and the European Foundation for the Improve- ment of Living and Working Conditions published the findings of research which identified community action as a constructive response to people's situations (Chanan and Vos, 1989). The emerging view from the increasing networks among community groups in European countries is that commun- ity work has a particular role to play in assisting in the reconstruction of local economies and social systems, as well as helping create closer social and community cohesion (Baine *et al.*, 1992; Harvey, 1992; McConnell, 1992). It is likely that further links will be made between countries in the European Union and it is possible that community work will have a role in assisting the invigoration of local communities. There are in place limited funds for community development from the European Social Fund and through the European Programme to Combat Poverty. There is concern, though, that these arrangements will exclude the needs of members of ethnic groups, who will become, as a group, the thirteenth [now the sixteenth] state of the European Union (Sondhi, 1994).

Economically, industry and commerce in the United Kingdom have con- tinued to suffer from problems of under-investment and a large trade imbal- ance with the rest of the world. According to many economists, the UK is paying the price of poor economic management during the 1980s. To quote the Economics Editor of the *Guardian*:

The sins of the fathers have truly been visited upon the sons. The 1980's, the decade of the economic miracle, was in reality 10 years of wild economic mismanagement and monstrous self-delusion. Britain over-consumed and under-produced to an astonishing degree and has been left with its finances – private, public and external – in such disarray that it may take the whole of the 1990's to recover. And even that is not certain.

(Hutton, 1993)

With official unemployment rates at around 2.5 million, but 'real' unemployment 1 million higher (Unemployment Unit and Youth Aid, 1993), new social and economic divisions, a growing elder and dependent population, and 'opting out' and contracting of local authority services, there appear to be fresh contemporary challenges for the activity known as community work.

Conclusion

This chapter has examined the development of community work and has demonstrated that the activity emerged from two main traditions, benevolent paternalism and collective community action, which have been present in various guises in different periods during its long history.

The activity received a major impetus in the 1960s from a series of international and national events and developments which recharged collective community action to assist in the organization of the poor in the challenge to economic inequality and social injustice. At the same time, community work became a state-sponsored method of stimulating welfare and education agencies to respond more effectively in what were termed 'pockets of deprivation'. This led to the 'golden age' of community work, with a rapid development during the 1970s in a wide range of activities and styles of working in both the statutory and voluntary sector.

The state became, and remains, the major funder of community work, although with the establishment of New Right philosophy and policies in the early 1980s community work found its scope, focus and direction determined by a rigid doctrine which clashed with the traditionally liberal, and in many cases socialist and radical, views and ideals of its practitioners. In the 1990s community work is dealing with the decline in the Urban Programme (which has been, since 1968, one of its major forms of funding). This, coupled with changes in the employment training schemes, has reduced community work activity.

Contemporary community work is therefore at a significant stage in its evolution which reflects the continuing tension between consensus and in some examples regressive practice, and collective community action. The dominance of the state in both community work's development and its present position demands a more detailed examination which continues in the following chapter.

Chapter 3

COMMUNITY WORK THEORY

Introduction

This chapter explores the nature of the different theories that inform community work. After a short discussion on the meaning of theory, the chapter reviews the community work literature and examines in more detail the discussion which began earlier on the different perspectives. It then continues with an evaluation of these theoretical debates.

What is theory?

The term 'theory' is an integral feature of social science investigation and is employed to explain social phenomena. However, the term itself is rarely examined. It is therefore important briefly to consider what the term means before exploring the various theories that underpin community work.

On a basic level humans not only 'do things' but also think about what they are doing. They attempt to make sense of their encounters with the world, to look for patterns and regularities in order to predict the outcome of their actions. Generally we seek to reduce the uncertainty in the material and social world by creating ideas and theories which are then tested and become established, the overall purpose being to create a greater understanding of the world which we inhabit and to make our encounters and interactions less threatening.

Although a theory is a system of ideas or statements that is held as an explanation for a group of facts or phenomena, theories themselves are neither totally objective nor ahistorical. For instance, the biological theories of race which were created in the nineteenth century claimed that it was possible to classify the different human 'races' by their physical characteristics, in particular skin colour. From this classification biologists argued that some 'races' were superior to others, and later in the century, under the influence of Darwin's theory of evolution, it was believed this difference was the consequence of the process of natural selection. These theories are now refuted, and are seen as attempts to support the view that white people are superior to black people. However, when the theories were in existence they were given powerful legitimation by white society which benefited from the results of these theories in practice.

Theories, therefore, have to be treated with caution and understood as a feature of the society and the period in which they are located. With this in mind we can now examine the theories that are discussed in the community work literature.

Community work theories

There have been a number of reviews of the development of theory in British community work (see, for example, Bryers, 1979; Hanmer and Rose, 1980; Tasker, 1980; Thomas, 1983). These studies conclude that there is no distinct community work theory, rather a clutch of theories which can broadly be divided into categories related to macro-theories of society. The categories used in this work are: pluralist theories; radical and socialist theories; feminist theories; and the black and anti-racist critique.

Pluralist community work theories

As we observed in Chapter 1, pluralist theories have dominated the debate around modern community work since the early 1960s. Furthermore, as we noted in both Chapters 1 and 2, pluralism is an integral aspect of social-democratic politics which was in the ascendancy during the post-war period.

Pluralist theories, which have been strongly influenced by Schumpeter (1976) and Weber (1930; 1978), argue that power in society is not located in any single group or type of group. Instead, within democracy, all public policies are the outcome of compromises between different competing groups. The theories claim that no group that wishes to affect outcomes lacks the necessary resources, and each may therefore be effective on some issues. These competing interest groups or factions are seen as vital to democracy and stability because they divide power and prevent any one group or class exerting an exclusive influence. This continual bargaining between the numerous interest groups in society means they all have some impact on policy. According to pluralists, the state has a role in balancing these different competing interests and ensuring that political decision-making takes account of the range of views expressed by the electorate.

In relation to community work, pluralist theories suggest a role that is active in supporting and encouraging participation in the political and administrative processes as a means of increasing the accessibility and accountability of services. Historically, pluralist theories have been linked with mainstream social administration, with their concern for intervention in the shape of piecemeal reforms and the amelioration of social problems. The role of community work in this paradigm is to help various groups to overcome the problems they face in their neighbourhoods or community often by mutual support, sharing activities, and by attempting to secure better services for their members.

One of the early attempts to develop a community work practice theory in Britain was Batten (1967), whose work was based on pluralist theories. A former community development worker in ex-colonies, Batten constructed an educational approach that aimed at personal growth. This practice theory argued that by working towards people's self-direction and responsibility it was possible for them to change their attitudes and responses which in turn would lead to an improvement in their material conditions. This approach, which informed much of the early community work training, was later to come under heavy criticism from the radical approach.

As we registered in Chapter 1, the practice theories of community work based on a pluralist analysis have been developed over the years by a number of writers, including Biddle and Biddle (1965), Goetschius (1975), Henderson and Thomas (1987), Leaper (1971), Thomas (1983) and Twelvetrees (1991). Thomas, for instance, argues that community work is a pluralist occupation and that the political differences that exist within community worker groups are a strength, but that 'we need to create the organisational and conceptual basis around which differences might cohere within a reasonably evident occupational identity' (Thomas, 1983: 16). Later he describes community work as a 'public service occupation, with a discernible set of skills and knowledge' (Thomas, 1983: 231).

Although primarily concerned with theories of community work practice as opposed to 'grand theories' of society, the pluralist approach nevertheless acknowledges the structural nature of deprivation and recognizes the political dimension to community work. The focus, however, is on micro-change, since advocates of this approach believe that community work is concerned with social consensus and marginal improvements, and hence they emphasize the value of its educational and experimental aspects. In this context education is seen as a means of 'enhancing political responsibility', the equipping of groups and individuals for effective participation, and, to quote one of its main exponents, 'the promotion and maintenance of communal coherence – the repair of social networks, the awakening of consciousness and responsibility for others and the creation of roles and functions that provide individual significance and a social service' (Thomas, 1983: 97). Pluralist theories lay considerable stress upon the importance of skills, and although recognizing the centrality of values, good practice is defined in terms of technical competence rather than conformance with any particular set of values: 'We suggest that there are identifiable skills and techniques which can be used in a multiplicity of situations regardless of the value stance of workers or neighbourhood groups' (Henderson and Thomas, 1987: 28).

An example of pluralist community work theory

Skills in Neighbourhood Work (Henderson and Thomas, 1987) is not only a 'how-to-do-it' text but also a clear exposition of the pluralist approach to community work. It emphasizes the need to focus on the neighbourhood because this is where people are increasingly spending their time due to changes in work patterns including unemployment; demographic changes; and policy initiatives, for instance the move from institutional care to community care. The authors argue that there exists a poverty of neighbourhood theory due to the emphasis within community work on the 'vertical relationships between community groups and resource holders' rather than 'an interest in community interaction' (Henderson and Thomas, 1987: 5). As we will see later, this is clearly a critical reference to the radical and socialist approaches to community work. The text supports the view that neighbourhoods need professional workers skilled in working with people to achieve what the authors describe as 'community capability'. Henderson and Thomas write with a view to encouraging other professionals, including social workers, youth workers and education workers, as well as community development workers, to adopt neighbourhood-based work. The purpose of the text therefore is to assist community workers, and in particular neighbourhood workers, in developing a repertoire of skills and knowledge to accomplish a wide range of tasks.

Radical and socialist community work theories

As we noted earlier, the late 1960s and early 1970s witnessed the emergence of community work theories based upon radical and socialist thinking. Radical theories of society have traditionally advocated far-reaching and fundamental changes in the political, social and economic system. A radical has been described as someone 'who proposes to attack some political or social problem by going deep into the socio-economic fabric to get at the fundamental or root cause and alter this basic social weakness' (Robertson, 1985: 80). Radical theories include anarchism, which is based on the proposition that society can operate without a government, and that governments are only legitimate if they are truly consented to by the individuals they govern. Anarchism advocates the establishment and the operation of voluntary associations based on co-operative principles and mutual aid. Radical theories, including anarchism, have often been associated with the far left in the political spectrum, and are used as such in the context here. However, it should be noted that it is possible to talk in political terms of the radical centre and the radical right, and to recognize that anarchists have been associated with the far right. Finally, Fromm (1969) believes radicalism need not relate to a set of ideas but to an attitude or approach where everything is questioned or doubted.

Socialism, on the other hand, has come to mean a variety of different things. At its most basic it is a political-economic system where the state controls, to a greater or less degree, the means of production in order to produce what is necessary for and needed by society without regard to the desire to obtain a profit. The central features of socialism include the creation of a just and egalitarian society, the removal of poverty, and the establishment of a particular moral system. Internationally, socialism as a political ideal is underpinned by a Marxist critique of capitalism. In the United Kingdom, socialism is a mixture of both Fabianism and Marxism. Fabianism, which dates from 1884 and which has always been closely related to the Labour Party, has traditionally advocated a peaceful political progress to socialism, through electoral politics. According to George and Wilding (1985: 94) Fabianism views the welfare state as a 'potential stepping stone toward socialism', although the same writers comment that there is a recognition that this hinges on the balance of economic and political forces in society.

The radical and socialist theories emerged within community work in the late 1960s and were part of the activity's 'golden age'. These theories were used by community workers to understand inequality within society, and the disadvantage experienced by a range of individuals and groups. As Britain's manufacturing base declined, particularly in older industrial and inner-city areas, and while rapid industrial change occurred elsewhere, working-class communities began to experience great difficulties. This led community workers to advocate and develop community action which supported groups and communities in conflict with authority. In a seminal paper on the origins of the radical trend within community work, Baldock (1977) argues that radicals and socialists were able to put into practice their developing theories because of: the expansion of community work during the 1960s and 1970s; the ideological influences and the political and social upheaval in the late 1960s, which encouraged critical rethinking of consensus and conservative views of society (both these points were discussed in Chapter 2); and the receptivity of 'target areas' for more radical community work practice, especially in projects related to slum clearance. Community work practice that has been informed by these theories has traditionally been undertaken by community activists who have employed a class analysis and the rhetoric and pursuance of class struggle at both a local and regional level. These theories have encouraged community work activity outside state funding, although one of the most notable examples of community workers using radical and socialist theories were those employed in the state-funded Community Development Projects.

Later, the work of Gough (1979) and the London Edinburgh Weekend Return Group (1980) tried to apply Marxist political economy to an analysis of the welfare state. These indicated the contradictory nature of the welfare state and its contradictory impact upon capitalism. The authors argue that the welfare state contains policies that can be defended and extended, while recognizing, exposing and attacking its negative aspects. In this way, they argue, 'welfare capitalism' can be transformed to 'welfare socialism'. These theories have led radical and socialist community workers to recognize the value of engaging in the activity as state-funded employees and trying to find the oppositional space to undertake successfully work that sustains a struggle against the state. This has been described as a 'progressive form of practice' (Bolger *et al.*, 1981: 144).

In more recent years the recognition that socialism as a system has 'failed' in the Soviet Union and eastern Europe, and the failure of Marx's predictions and revolutions in the advanced, industrialized societies of the West, has posed a dilemma for advocates of the ideal. Whether socialism will again attract the appeal it did in the past is uncertain, although, as Scase (1992) has indicated, Marxist theory continues to be relevant in contemporary society, providing us with a valuable critique of industrial capitalism.

An example of radical and socialist community work theory

Discussion in Chapters 1 and 2 indicated that the Community Development Projects were the clearest example of the radical and socialist approaches to community work. Rejecting their conservative origins, the Community Development Projects developed a Marxist structuralist analysis of social deprivation and argued that community work could function as a mechanism for social control. The Community Development Projects' contribution to the development of community work theory has been much debated, with Thomas (1983) criticizing their 'doctrinaire style' and continuous devaluation of neighbourhood work which, he argues, alienated practitioners and inhibited open discussion. On the other hand, Henderson (1983) and Waddington (1983) argue that the Community Development Projects filled an ideological and theoretical vacuum, bringing a necessary coherence to community work. At the theoretical level there is little doubt that the Community Development Projects offered a radical break with earlier traditions, and that their analysis has had a major impact not only upon community work but also within the arenas of social policy and local and central government. The strength of their arguments, Henderson (1983: 7) suggests, lay in the quality of their analysis which was grounded in careful local investigation and the reality of working-class experience, and their 'insistence on social class as the fundamental tool for understanding the areas where many community workers were employed'. In relation to practice it is harder to determine the influence of Community Development Projects. The problem, Waddington (1983: 42) suggests, lies partly in the fact that 'many community workers have found it difficult to operationalise or apply [radical] theory to their own practice, partly because the material produced by the Community Development Projects has tended to be longer on analysis than applications'.

According to Thomas (1983), the Community Development Projects' attack on the value of neighbourhood work had a demoralizing effect on many workers at the time, undermining their faith and confidence in the potential of community work to effect social change. On a more positive note, their recognition of the importance of linking community and workplace struggles and the location of community work within a wider social analysis, which recognized the relationship between the economy and welfare provision, was invaluable. However, the Community Development Projects have been criticized by feminists for being gender-blind, and by black writers and anti-racist activists as being 'colour'-blind. Both groups have criticized the Community Development Projects, as well as the Left in general, for marginalizing their contributions and ignoring their experiences. Nevertheless, by rooting community work firmly in a structuralist analysis the projects established the radical and socialist approach on a firm theoretical foundation.

Socialist and radical theories, based upon a theory of class, are now less in evidence in community work than they were in the 1970s. There has, however, been an upsurge in two significant strands of these theories that do not necessarily have class as its main focus: feminist theories; and the black and anti-racist critique.

Feminist community work theories

The emergence of feminist theory, and in particular socialist feminist theory, during the 1970s, prompted a re-evaluation of the male-dominated radical and socialist community work theory and practice. This is discussed by, among others, Hanmer and Rose (1980) who point out that women, particularly those with young children, represent the key constituency for community work. The authors argue therefore that if community workers are to 'start where people are at', they have to take account of and relate to the experience of women's oppression.

At a theoretical level, socialist feminists have demonstrated the inadequacy of a Marxist structuralist approach in explaining women's oppression. While traditional gender assumptions benefit capitalism, socialist feminist theory has demonstrated that men derive real material benefits from women's unpaid work at home and in the community and thus have a vested interest in perpetuating the position of women. Declaring that the 'personal is political' (Millet, 1969), feminist theory and practice stress the political element in personal relationships and highlight the need to link home, workplace and the community (Land, 1980; Lewis, 1986; McIntosh, 1981; Pascall, 1986; Williams, 1989; Wilson, 1982; 1983; 1986). While emphasizing the importance of personal experience in developing links between women, feminist writers and workers have also stressed the centrality of personal experience and self-disclosure as a focus for work with women in the community (for example, Barker, 1986; Finch, 1982; Freeman, 1984). By highlighting the importance of personal experience, feminist theory argues that while women may experience oppression differently and often individually, they share a common interest which inevitably influences the way they work and the issues they choose to work on. However, Smithies and Webster (1987) caution that common interests should not be used to advocate some utopian ideal of sisterhood. They argue that differences cannot and should not be minimalized or accommodated but instead could provide a starting point for the development of creative practical action for change. It was in the context of the above that consciousness-raising groups emerged in Britain as a means of encouraging the reflection and action necessary for personal change and possible political transformation (Rowbotham, 1979).

Feminist theory, including socialist feminist analysis, has been criticized by black feminists who argue that such theories tend to marginalize black women and to render them invisible through a failure to account for their simultaneous oppressions by patriarchy, by class and by race. Further, the challenge to these failings lies in the questioning of categories and assumptions which are central to what is regarded as 'mainstream feminist thought' – specifically, white, middle-class feminist conceptualizations of patriarchy, the family and reproduction – which is rendered problematic when imposed upon the lives of black women (Bryan *et al.*, 1985; Mama, 1989; Ng, 1988; Yurval, 1992). Black feminists within community work have struggled to put their theories into practice, often against a reaction both from other women and the state (Bhavnani, 1982). Black feminists also maintain that black men similarly suffer from racism and on this central issue align themselves together.

The work of Ware (1991), however, does attempt to link the history of anti-racist and anti-slavery struggles with those of feminists. Ware argues that the relationship between feminism and the black struggle has been overlooked, yet both are engaged in an attempt to achieve equality and in a resistance against forms of oppression. Ware (1991: xiv) suggests theoretical possibilities towards 'finding a language that would express the links between race and gender, without prioritising and without oversimplifying ... to work out ways of resisting one form of domination without being complicated in another'.

The black and anti-racist community work critique

Just as socialist and radical feminist theory has highlighted the need to reconstruct classical Marxist theory in the light of women's experience, so also the black and anti-racist critique emphasizes the interrelation between race and class, and to a lesser extent gender (Amin and Leech, 1988; Bhat *et al.*, 1988; Braham *et al.*, 1992; Gilroy, 1987; Gordon, 1989; Sivanandan, 1990).

In line with the literature on 'race' and racism, the term 'critique' is used here instead of 'theory'. The black and anti-racist critique, which draws from black radicalism, from socialism and Marxism, and from black feminism, argues that white people benefit from racism and the oppression of black people within contemporary Britain. Demonstrating that Western capitalism is built on the foundations of the slavery and imperialism from which it derived its wealth and power, the critique argues that this domination is perpetuated in the 'Third World' through trade, aid and foreign debt. The critique claims that within Britain, state policy has operated as a repressive force on black people particularly in relation to immigration policy and law and order policy (Coleman, 1987; Dummett, 1986; Genders and Player, 1990; Hiro, 1992; McDermott, 1990; National Association for the Care and Resettlement of Offenders, 1988; National Association of Probation Officers, 1988; Runnymede Trust, 1992). On a broader scale, there is a recognition within the critical social sciences that racism operates at a personal and an institutional level as a material and ideological force permeating major institutions in society. Work by Bryan *et al.* (1985), Mama (1989) and Williams (1989) further demonstrates the racist nature of the administration of welfare benefits and services and how black people's labour and resources were essential in creating the British welfare state.

In relation to community work there have been two constant themes within this critique. One has been the resistance to racism, which Ohri *et al.* (1982) point out remains the primary issue for the black community, and one which community work must address if it is to remain relevant to the needs and concerns of black people. The other major theme has been the opportunities community work has provided to different groups to encourage cultural formations in their own right.

> In a highly complex and interwoven system of cultural overlap, black people have sustained and generated cultures and formations that not only react to discrimination and inequality but also create processes that have an identity and vitality of their own, independent of hostility from the dominant group.
>
> (Popple, 1990: 137)

Evaluating community work theories

We have noted that although there is no one community work theory, the activity has been influenced by a number of macro-theories. Since the mid 1970s, community work advocates of these macro-theories have not enjoyed the smoothest of relationships, mainly because the advocates of socialist, radical, feminist theories and the black and anti-racist critique, which have shared critical perspectives, have been at variance with advocates of the pluralist theories. During the early 1970s the socialist and radical theories of social, political and economic change came to challenge the dominant pluralist theories, leading to what one writer describes as a 'problematic discourse' between the main approaches to community work (Twelvetrees, 1991: 5).

It has been argued here that pluralist theories have resulted in the establishment of acceptable practice methods in order to handle state-defined prevailing social problems experienced in communities. This then assists in the efficiency and profitability of a social-democratic market economy. The chosen form of social intervention is based on technical skills which can be at the expense of a critical appreciation of a changing social, economic and political world, or a commitment to being part of significant change within society. We have noted that by concentrating on the marginal gains possible, pluralist community work theory can fail to make effective theoretical and practical connections between individuals' experience and the changing nature of society. Clearly pluralist theory involves value judgements, and although pluralist community work theories have never claimed to be value-free, we should be aware that its theories and practice values are not exposed fully, and therefore result in an aura of neutrality and objectivity. Another criticism of pluralist community work theory is that because of its focus on the neighbourhood it fails to connect sufficiently with the production and reproduction of inequalities in the wider society which result in problems for localities.

Pluralist theories also emphasize the view that collective, social and insti-tutionalized policies can stem only from government action or from the work of major community work agencies. This omits an appreciation of the unpaid army of people (usually women) who are engaged in, and have developed, community work practice. Pluralist community work theory tends to reflect the view that producing evidence on social problems will prompt a social conscience response. Its empiricist emphasis on the collec-tion of 'facts', rather than on theory-building, gives credence to the view that piecemeal reform and intervention are possible and can be quantified or measured. A further criticism of the pluralist community work theories is that community work tends to placate rather than liberate the individuals and groups that come within its orbit. It is something that is 'done to' rather than determined by a community. In this paradigm community work is viewed as a professional and arguably elitist activity, undertaken by paid workers on behalf of agencies rather than by those living in a particular community. The reference group is the employing agency, not the community. Meanwhile pluralist community work theories often promote the concept of self-help and self-reliance, a concept that appeals to a wide political spectrum. It is a concept favoured by those who believe in an individualist/*laissez-faire* approach as well as those holding an anarchist, anti-statist view. The purpose of self-help here, however, is not to liberate a community, but to marshal 'commun-ity energies to replace public services rather than complement them' (Taylor, 1992: 18).

On a more positive note, the pluralist approach has offered community work a range of practice theories and practical 'how-to-do-it' guidelines which are acceptable to practitioners of most ideological positions working in a wide range of statutory and voluntary bodies. In this way community work has come to influence other forms of practice in the public service, including social work and education.

Community work theories which have evolved from classical Marxist theories associated in practice with the class-orientated community action of the Community Development Projects, have come to challenge the pluralist community work theories. These analyses have influenced not only the type of constituent groups worked with, but also the form of working and the values and principles that shape the community work being undertaken. These relatively recent developments in community work theory have been underpinned and influenced by the growing macro-theoretical work which offers critical explanations about social phenomena.

The socialist community work theories provide an analysis of society which is a mixture of idealism and materialism. The idealism derives from the Fab-ian socialist tradition which, as we noted earlier, believes that it is possible to achieve change through rational discourse, the fostering of collective values and moral persuasion. This idealism is evident, for instance, in the belief that it is possible to prevent sexism or racism by educating people to act and think differently. Fabian socialism has been criticized by a number of writers, including Williams, who argues that it 'fails to recognize the bearing that society itself has on the creation and sustenance of ideas' (Williams, 1989: 22).

This leads one to consider the notion of materialism. Marxists have demonstrated that ideas are inextricably linked to daily life. According to such theorists, ideas are shaped around the conflicts of interests between capital and labour, leading to struggle and change. In this paradigm capital accommodates change and conflict. One of the problems of this materialist understanding is that it fails to recognize the resistance that comes from the grassroots and the potential for change that can come through resistance to an all-powerful hegemony. It is this materialist view that has been criticized by others on the left who perceive the possibilities for change.

The main criticism that can be levelled at the radical and socialist theories is that practice by itself cannot change society. Socialism is both a political doctrine and a political movement containing a view of human action, and a vision of human potential that is in essence internationalist or universal. 'Left' radicalism, on the other hand, offers a far-reaching critique of society that questions the very nature of the social, political and economic forces within society but does not offer a comprehensive and workable view of a future society. Both radical and socialist theories can lead to action in a whole range of fields, community work being one minute segment. In order to achieve socialist goals, for instance, change has to be enacted at every level of society. Community workers, however, work with a small and relatively powerless section of the population, and although practitioners influenced by socialist theories may attempt to 'prefigure' a more just and equal society they will not alone achieve large-scale change. On a wider level, we have noted that the 'fall of socialism' in eastern Europe and the former Union of Soviet Socialist Republics has led to questions of whether a Marxist materialist position can successfully be put in place.

Feminist theory and the black and anti-racist critique, have, on the other hand, demonstrated that all oppressed groups, and in this case, women and black people, can, through collective action, attempt to overcome their subordination. Feminism, both as a socio-political theory and as a social movement, has, for instance, reconstructed perspectives in many different areas of life. Together, feminist theory and the black and anti-racist critique have implications for community work theory that do not rely on either localized analysis or materialist perspectives.

One of the main criticisms that can be levelled at both the pluralist and the radical and socialist community work theories is that the debates between the two major approaches have been both insular and specific. It can be argued that these debates were useful and important to the emerging profession in the 1970s, but since then these debates have been rather isolated from a literature that offers community work opportunities to examine its role and ideology alongside key developments in critical theory. The criticism of insularity is far less true of feminist and of black and anti-racist literature, which has demonstrated that it is possible to draw from other significant sources. The literature on which community work can now draw is located in political science, social theory and sociology. In the next chapter we will discuss these broader theories and consider their implications for community work theory.

Chapter 4

COMMUNITY WORK THEORY: THE WAY FORWARD?

Introduction

The previous chapter reviewed the main theories that have informed community work, highlighting their strengths and weaknesses. We have noted that one of the main criticisms that can be levelled at the pluralist, radical and socialist community work theories is that the debates between the two major approaches have been insular and specific. These debates were useful and important to the emerging profession in the 1970s, but since then have failed sufficiently to assist our demand to understand the changing nature of the activity.

The purpose of this chapter is to examine the role of community workers in a wider context. To do this consideration is given to the writings of the Italian social theorist, Antonio Gramsci, whose work offers an understanding of the role state workers such as community workers can play in assisting communities. These ideas were first developed in an article in a previously published community work volume (Popple, 1994). The chapter will then move to discuss a number of theories that relate to urban and social movements which similarly can be considered to have much to offer community work theory.

The writings of Antonio Gramsci: their contribution to community work

Karl Marx's theories produced a clear vision of social change by detailing the inevitable succession of the bourgeoisie by the proletariat. The increasing complexity of social life in the twentieth century, however, denied Marx's vision as willing and unwilling concessions from the dominant class to the subordinate classes and groups, and the failure of revolution to change the nature of the state, undermined his analysis. The Italian social theorist, Antonio Gramsci (1891–1937), recognized the inadequacy of this economic determinism and instead focused on key aspects of Marx's Hegelian, humanistic theory to reconceptualize the moral, philosophical and political spheres of social life. Gramsci provided an expanded vision of politics, one that moves away from a concept of politics as being about electoral politics, narrow party politics or the occupancy of state power. Instead Gramsci perceives politics as a struggle for moral and intellectual leadership. To quote Hall (1988: 169):

> Where Gramsci departs from classical versions of Marxism is that he does not think that politics is an arena which simply rejects already unified collective political identities, already constituted forms of struggle. Politics for him is not a dependent sphere. It is where forces and relations, in the economy, in society, in culture, have to be actively worked on to produce particular forms of domination. This is the production of politics – politics as a production. This conception of politics is fundamentally open-ended.

One of the most positive aspects of Gramsci's work is its rejection of crude historical materialist analysis. This type of analysis was typical of the Marxist Left in the 1960s and 1970s which influenced the Community Development Projects and the radical and socialist community workers of the period. Instead, Gramsci's work provides us with an analysis of how groups and individuals can shape developments within society. Here his concepts of hegemony, ideology and intellectuals are the most relevant.

Gramsci (1971; 1975; 1977; 1978) discusses the notion that any ruling elite dominates subordinate classes and groups with a combination of force and consent. He argued that force is exercised through the armed forces, the police, the law courts and prisons, while consent is gained through the political, moral and intellectual leadership within civil society. This domination is maintained by a process of hegemony which has been described as

> the relation between classes and other social forces. A hegemonic class, or part of a class, is one which gains the consent of other classes and social forces through creating and maintaining a system of alliance by means of political struggle.
>
> (Simon, 1982: 22)

Gramsci argues that the civil society, which has been defined by Gramscians as consisting of organizations such as political parties, trade unions, churches and cultural, charitable and community groups, is central in sustaining the hegemony. According to Gramscians, civil society is the sphere where popular-democratic struggles are grouped together – race, gender, age, community, ethnicity, nation and so forth – and that it is here that the struggle for hegemony takes place. These struggles have been identified as social movements, and we will return to them later.

To achieve an effective hegemony, Gramsci argued, there must be a number of beliefs or ideas which are generally accepted by all but which serve to justify the interests of the dominant groups. These images, concepts and ideas which 'make sense' of everyday experiences are collectively known as 'ideology'. Gramsci argues that ideology is the cement that keeps society together. According to Sayer (1986), any change in ideology has to be undertaken at the institutional level. However, Gramsci also argues that the subordinate classes or groups do not necessarily have the conceptual tools to comprehend the situation fully, or the means to formulate the radical alternatives to change the ideology or overcome the hegemonic forces. If change is to take place, Gramsci believes that 'external agents', in the guise of intellectuals, organizers and leaders, are necessary. Gramsci's definition of 'intellectuals' extends beyond the traditionally held notion of thinkers, philosophers, artists, journalists and writers, to include organizers such as civil servants and political leaders who are active in civil society, as well as engineers, managers and technicians who function in the production sphere. Gramsci describes 'organic' intellectuals as those who have been created by a particular class and 'give it homogeneity and an awareness of its own function not only in the economic but also in the social and political fields' (Gramsci, 1971: 5). These intellectuals are members of the class they represent. Thus a dominant class creates its own intellectuals in the form of economists, civil servants, industrial managers, writers and media personnel who reflect and support the values of that class.

Returning to our consideration of community work, are community workers 'organic' intellectuals? Most practitioners are employed in one way or another by the state and are therefore acting with particular instructions or authority, so that they could be considered to be a subordinate branch of the dominant 'organic' intellectuals. On the other hand, the fact that they can be at odds with the dominant ideology and are encouraging individuals and groups to articulate their own discourse means they do not fully agree with the dominant system. Therefore, it could be interpreted that community workers are strategic players in helping people make connections between their position and the need for change.

To help us in understanding and clarifying the role of community workers in this paradigm we can again refer to Simon (1982), who argues that certain groups of workers are part of an important 'middle stratum' which has particular professional and corporate interests and traditions. Simon believes it is the specialized training provided in institutions such as colleges which separates the 'middle stratum' from the vast majority of workers.

They have been constituted into a variety of 'middle strata' capable of playing a distinctive part in politics which can be very significant indeed. They are therefore a vital component of the broad alliance which has to be built up by the working class if it is to achieve a hegemonic role in society.

(Simon, 1982: 98)

Gramsci and Simon demonstrate, however, that members of this 'middle stratum' can hold traditional views and act as instruments of political stability. For instance, Gramsci is critical of the conservative role adopted by trade unions and their leaders in working within bourgeois democracy. Similarly, he argues that the economic and political system does not represent the non-elite and consequently there is always the potential for social disintegration. What can be drawn from these observations is that community workers have a role in facilitating the response of the non-elite and a role in the changing of social circumstances.

Aspects of Gramsci's theories, then, offer us a workable framework for our examination of community work theory. His theories reject the notion of class agents as the sole bearers of change, and more importantly the concept of one hegemonic centre in society. Dominant groups maintain and reproduce their ascendancy through a complex web of ideological processes in an attempt to establish an agreed understanding of reality. This understanding of reality is intended to permeate our principles, social relationships and intellectual and moral positions. However, according to Gramscians this understanding is never completely secure because our daily experiences of the world are frequently at odds with the view offered by bourgeois ideology. We can, therefore, simultaneously hold different and apparently contradictory and inconsistent interpretations of the world – one determined and shaped by the prevailing dominant ideology, and the other determined by our everyday experiences in communities which gives us 'common-sense' knowledge. In this paradigm community workers are situated in a pivotal position within the civil society, for although they are employees of the state and are required to play a part in maintaining the social system, they are not necessarily in agreement with its ideology. Accordingly, community workers have opportunities to work alongside members of communities as they articulate their contradictory understanding of the world and their situation within it (see Figure 4.1). This theory also proposes that community work is concerned with moving from the terrain of ideas and discussion and into transforming action to change people's material situation, which we will discuss below.

Freed from the boundaries of Marxism and the economic determinist position, Gramsci's theoretical work allows us to develop concepts that enable us to locate community work within a site of resistance. These developing Gramscian concepts and the complementary analysis provided by a number of social theorists further enable us to trace a theoretical basis for the emergence of urban social movements and new social movements. These can be seen as strategies of resistance to old and new forms of oppression.

The potential contribution of the study of social movements to community work theory

In the discussion in Chapter 3 we noted a degree of insularity in the development of community work theories. As a result of this insularity, community

Figure 4.1 Hegemony and the sphere of popular-democratic struggle

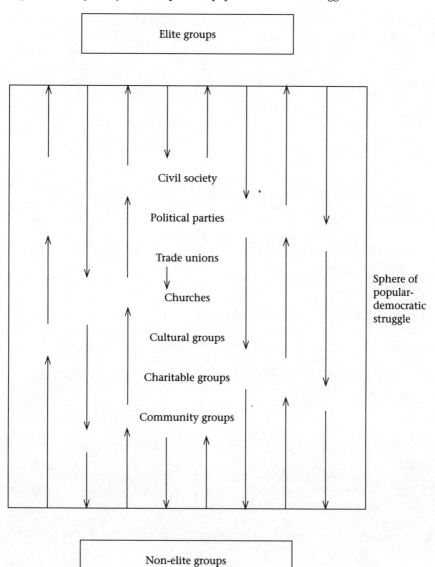

Elite groups

Civil society

Political parties

Trade unions

Churches

Cultural groups

Charitable groups

Community groups

Sphere of
popular-
democratic
struggle

Non-elite groups

work theories have failed to draw from useful analysis elsewhere. One such important area is the substantial literature addressing urban social movements and new social movements which themselves have been a popular subject of sociological investigation. We have seen from our examination of the work of Gramsci that a specific contribution to community work theory can be derived from sources outside the specific literature relating to its practice. However, a study of social movements similarly offers opportunities to make connections with theories concerning the nature and motivation of collective action.

Before progressing, it is important to distinguish between urban social movements and new social movements. Urban social movements have been described as

> organisations, which bring people together to defend or challenge the provision of urban public services and protect the local environment. The implication of these organisations as 'social movements' is that their objectives are undertaken collectively by the mobilisation of a distinct social base and that the momentum of their activity is towards changes in policy direction.
>
> (Lowe, 1986: 3)

Similarly, Dunleavy (1980: 156) believes that a central feature of urban social movements is their 'organizing around urban issues of collective consumption'.

In Britain, urban social movements have more usually been described as a form of community action, for example: squatters movements; community groups organizing against road-widening and road-building schemes; tenants' groups opposing rent rises, organizing for better repair systems, and, during the late 1980s, protesting against the 1988 Housing Act; together with a whole range of groups opposing public expenditure reductions in education, health and social security. Urban social movements do not necessarily have to be left-wing, as was seen in the mid-1970s when ratepayers' organizations emerged to advocate the abolition of rates and promote private sector provision of urban services. A further example during the late 1980s was the North Downs Rail Concern Action Group which protested against the proposed routes for the Channel Tunnel's high-speed rail link. The majority of its members were middle-class owner-occupiers who resided in Conservative-controlled county councils and were represented by Conservative MPs (Phillips, 1989).

New social movements, like urban social movements, are also collective attempts to further a common interest or goal outside the sphere of established institutions. New social movements, however, are primarily social and, according to A. Scott (1990), their focus is on values and lifestyles. Since the late 1960s a wide variety of new social movements has emerged, the first major one in Britain being the student movement. During the same period a re-emergence took place of previous social movements. For instance, 'second-wave feminism' emerged, which was a revival of previous attempts to protect and extend women's rights. Similarly, the black civil rights movement gathered momentum in the United States. This movement had connections with a history of resistance to racism dating from previous centuries.

The dividing line between urban social movements and new social movements is blurred. For instance, squatting can be interpreted as direct action around the urban issue of collective consumption, in this case housing. It can therefore be argued that squatting is an urban social movement. At the same time, attempts by squatters to create or experiment with an alternative type of lifestyle, which may be linked to a network of other groups or even a mass movement of squatters, can lead one to describe these developments as a new social movement. There are, however, differences between the two types of social movement which we will explore in our discussion below.

The theories relating to social movements that are of particular assistance to our discussion of community work theory relate to collective consumption in the case of the urban social movements, and to the linking of micro-interventions to macro-movements in the example of new social movements.

Urban social movements

With regard to the theories relating to collective consumption, we need to examine the work of Manuel Castells, who, writing from an initially neo-Marxist position, argued that urban problems are a direct result of the relationship between capitalism and urbanism. Like other Marxists, he sees the production process as being at the heart of capitalism, with the city or communities as the site of the process of the reproduction of labour. Castells states that the reproduction of labour power has gradually become mediated through collective rather than individual means which have brought with them a series of contradictions which may, in time, cause a 'revolutionary rupture' in society. According to Castells, the major contradiction lies in the needs of capital and the need to reproduce labour. Private capital by itself cannot provide for the state's citizens and has therefore to intervene on a large scale in the area of housing, health care, education, public transport and so on. The state's intervention, however, highlights the economic contradiction. 'It globalizes and politicises all the problems in making their collective treatment more necessary and visible but at the same time in making their confrontation by the individual more difficult' (Castells, 1975: 190). This contradiction paves the way for a 'dialectic between the state apparatus, and urban social movement' (Castells, 1977: 463).

During the period in which Castells was writing he moved from a Leninist position, which argued that any social movement aimed at benefiting from these contradictions had to make organizations central to their response, to a position that highlights the feature of class recomposition in an increasingly divided and diversified social world. Castells change of position should, according to Lowe (1986), be interpreted not as a dismissal of the nature of class or its importance in social movements, but rather as a recognition that the interests of emerging powerful groupings, such as women and black people, can at times cut across class divides, as well as noting that the interests of different social classes do at certain points coincide.

The Weberian sociologists Pickvance (1977) and Saunders (1983) scrutinize the work of Castells and question whether urban movements can forge a popular alliance against the state and capital. Saunders, in his case against Castells, provides an example of the shortage of housing which may create conflict between the homeless and owner-occupiers even though both are drawn from the non-capitalist classes. The crisis in the provision of the collective means of consumption drives a wedge between groups, rather than bringing them together. Saunders argues that although housing is a collective provision, deprivation is experienced individually. Individuals on a council housing list perceive their position in terms of an individual problem and do not necessarily consider they are part of a collective response to, say, a rent rise. Collective action is therefore 'usually specific, short-lived and far from solid' (Saunders, 1983: 125). So although a crisis in collective consumption can generate social movements based upon issues of public transport, public health and education, where the issue 'is politicised by virtue of the role of the state and collectivised by virtue of the nature of facility' (Saunders, 1983: 126) this is more difficult in relation to housing which is the largest and, arguably, the most important of all urban responses. This leads Saunders to conclude that contemporary urban politics is really concerned with pressure groups which do not by themselves provide any great base for the development of political alliances, with protests remaining focused upon specific limited issues. These, he argues, have 'little significance for any future transition to a qualitatively different mode of organization of society' (Saunders, 1983: 136).

The implications here for community work theory are twofold. One is the recognition that urban problems are not neighbourhood-specific; they are a result of the way in which society is organized. Whether one chooses to adopt a neo-Marxist position and view these problems as due to capitalism, or the Weberian approach that perceives them as a result of urbanism *per se*, they both register the need for society to collectivize consumption of certain services. Both positions recognize that community work is one particular activity required in its delivery of public services. The second implication for community work theory questions the impact of the activity. For Castells and neo-Marxists, collective consumption politicizes the contradiction that capitalism requires individuals to pursue wealth accumulation, while recognizing society's need for the reproduction of labour and social relations. The urban social movements, in their struggle for better and different services, are a response to this contradiction. Saunders and other Weberian sociologists recognize the role of urban social movements but question whether they can impact upon wider society. They argue that collective consumption can divide as well as unite people. Further, they claim that urban social movements are essentially locality-based and short-lived, and have little influence on social, political and economic relations.

New social movements

We have seen that a number of urban sociologists believe that urban social movements, which in Britain have historically come to mean movements dominated by white males, are limited in their ability to achieve radical or major change. Pickvance, Saunders and the later writings of Castells have recognized the inadequacies of an analysis based on a conventional view of class. In response Castells (1983), for instance, attempts to develop a theory of urban social change which celebrates the cultural diversity of urban life. Other significant developments have, however, taken place that are similar but different in nature to those described as urban social movements which we have recorded above; these have become known as new social movements.

New social movements are part of a coalition of loosely knit groups that stand in oppositional alliance to a whole sphere of developments that are taking place in society, and some are thought to have the potential for greater radical change than others (Hall, 1988; Hall and Jacques, 1989; A. Scott, 1990). They include a range of disaffected and emerging groups as well as those that have been in evidence since the early to mid-1960s. It is possible to identify the following new social movements: the women's movement; the nuclear disarmament movement; the Greens; welfare rights organizations; the gay and lesbian movement; anti-racist groups; groups for different ethnic and cultural backgrounds; and nationalist groups demanding a greater involvement in the running of their own affairs. Although these groups have national and even international profiles, they draw their strength from neighbourhood and city-based activity that links them with each other through publications, conferences, rallies, meetings, demonstrations and a variety of other initiatives. One of the major themes of new social movements is 'act locally, think globally'. Within the development of new social movements it is possible to detect a strong concern among their members to avoid being subsumed by political ideologies, and to define their own goals, limits and forms of action. Of prime importance appears to be a desire to organize around the mobilization of people within society, rather than for the seizure of power.

New social movements are a reaction to the failure of the conventional urban social movements and the political parties on the left to break out of conventional methods of organizing, as well as a response to a range of issues that demand direct action. New social movements, it has been argued, are at the forefront of responding to problems as they collide with people's everyday experiences. They are not only engaged in challenging the activity of the state and civil society in a variety of areas, but also involved in proposing and initiating alternatives. The women's movement has been particularly active in encouraging and developing alternative approaches to theory and practice in political organization. Women, who are frequently at the cornerstone of many new social movement developments, have made demands on such issues as equal pay, abortion and contraception, legal rights and protection against domestic violence, while offering a number of working theories and practices which challenge the culture of patriarchy. For example, the work by Rowbotham (1992) argues the need to bring together people's experience of organizing in order to replace the old forms of political structure which she and other feminists believe fail to respond to grassroots demands.

There are a number of implications regarding the theories of new social movements that relate to community work theory. As we have noted, they have come to challenge values at an individual and a societal level. Their use of consciousness raising and anti-discriminatory practice, and their participatory and unhierarchical approaches to organizing, are a central feature. This feature is also an aspect of community work which is associated with radical and socialist theories. Similarly, the deconstruction and reconstruction of language – for instance, the use of 'gay' for 'homosexual', 'black' for 'negro', 'woman' for 'girl' – is part of a new discourse that has roots within the new social movements. Paulo Freire and Michel Foucault have both highlighted the historical formation of cultural practices and discourses. Freire's work (which we discuss in Chapter 5) highlights how people have been silenced or 'denied their voice' and stresses the importance of dialogue in the struggle of people who wish to become 'beings of self'. Foucault (1988; 1989), meanwhile, has drawn attention to discourse and practice. For Foucault power is in our action not our heads. Fraser (1989: 25), discussing Foucault, claims he means that 'practices are more fundamental than belief systems when it comes to understanding the hold that power has on us'. According to Foucault, the acceptance of certain discourses comes to validate certain versions of the truth. The establishing of alternative discourses, like those that have emerged from the new social movements can, Foucault claims, help to break truth from the 'forms of hegemony' in which it operates.

A final implication of the new social movements for community work is the increased awareness that the traditional working class is only one prime agent of change in contemporary society. There is a realization that emancipatory potential can reside in a number of groups within society. Some of these will be located primarily in the white working class, while others will be drawn from varying class and cultural formations within society.

Urban social movements and new social movements: the lessons for community work theory

What can community work theory gain from the literature relating to social movements? Pickvance and Saunders, who appear to support the pluralist view of community work, argue that urban social movements or community action are little more than limited, small-scale reactions to problems of collective consumption. They argue that such responses do not provide real grounds for believing that from such a base it is possible to develop political alliances. However, new social movements which are not adequately addressed by such critics, demonstrate that tentative links can be made. For instance, links were made between the women's movement, the peace movement and the Greens as witnessed at the demonstrations against the use of the United States Air Force base at Greenham Common in Berkshire to site nuclear weapons during the 1980s. In 1993 links were made between the Greens, the women's movement and Charter 88 in protests against road-building (Vidal, 1993). We have seen that both forms of social movement derive their understandings by making connections between individuals' experience and the nature of contemporary society. The contention here is that Saunders's argument has failed to appreciate the cultural dimension of social action. Such action is both reactive and proactive as it attempts to develop new theories and practice. Community work, with its wealth of experience and skill in working in some of the poorest neighbourhoods has, it would appear, the potential to feed into the debates surrounding social movements.

The benefit for community work theory is an expanded understanding of the nature of macro-forces which shape and impinge upon individuals and communities. Similarly, an understanding of the literature and sociological theory relating to social movements provides a broad background which could inform the practice of community work but can also be tempered by an awareness of the useful existing community work theory.

Conclusion

We noted in Chapter 3 that it is not possible to talk of a unified community work theory, but rather a number of macro-theories which have served to underpin and assist community workers, and explain and develop their work. Perhaps one salient reason for this lack of a clear theoretical base is the unique way in which community work responds to specific local conditions, making it difficult to provide examples of work that can be generalized.

In reviewing the established theories we identified their strengths and weaknesses, concluding that, except in aspects of feminist community work theory and the black and anti-racist critique, these theories have failed fully to appreciate an important literature that offers community work a means of further theorizing and understanding its role and operation, while recognizing a wider remit. In this chapter we have drawn on the work of Gramsci and developments in the urban and new social movements to demonstrate that communities can be one specific site in the resistance to different hegemonies. The community worker usually locates her/himself with the oppressed or subordinate groups and is therefore sometimes seen as politically radical. In order to challenge existing power structures, this radicalism may require a variety of theoretical perspectives to respond to a variety of social hegemonies. The lessons from Gramsci and the new social movements is that the background assumptions that operate in social relations can be challenged. This has implications for community work practice. Firstly, this requires a flexible community work practice responsive to the local conditions in which the worker finds her/himself. The skills and settings for this practice are discussed in subsequent chapters. Secondly, while local task-orientated community work is progressing, wider developments, sometimes at a global level, are taking place. This needs to be recognized and appreciated if community work is to be more than the localized neighbourhood activity that is advocated by the pluralist theorists.

Chapter 5

MODELS OF COMMUNITY WORK

Introduction

The previous chapters have provided us with an evolving and critical understanding of community work. In Chapter 2 we discussed the emergence of community work from different roots and traditions, and against a number of wider changes in the Western world, as well as considering the activity in relation to, and as part of, the social, political and economic developments within British society. In Chapter 3 we went on to examine the various, often competing, theories that inform community work, recognizing that there is no one theory that meets with universal agreement. In Chapter 4 we examined different sociological theories and social movements that have, until now, played little part in underpinning a theoretical base for community work, but could, if used appropriately, offer us a more critical understanding of the practice. Throughout this work our discussions have recognized that community work comprises both theory and practice, and although they are inextricably linked, for our own purposes it is more productive initially to consider each of them separately. The focus of this chapter is to reflect upon the theoretical understandings already developed by analysing the models which constitute contemporary community work practice. This in turn helps to distinguish community work from other forms of intervention. In this way this chapter acts as a bridge between the theoretical debates of Chapters 3 and 4, and the examination of community work practice to be developed in Chapter 6.

An extensive review of the community work literature fails to provide an agreed number or the exact scope of different community work models.

What has been developed here, therefore, is a discussion that includes the models most readily agreed upon: community care, community organization, community development, social/community planning, community education and community action, together with models developed from feminist community work theory and the black and anti-racist critique which were discussed in Chapter 3. It will be noted that these models have evolved often in an uncoordinated manner to address a particular difficulty or concern, or as the application of a particular theory or approach. It needs to be recognized that aspects of these models are not entirely discrete, but rather there is a degree of overlap between them. The models are, however, an important method of categorizing central approaches to the activity we call 'community work'. They have been ordered on a continuum from those concerned primarily with 'care' to those known for their emphasis on 'action'. This provides a helpful way of contrasting and comparing the models. Table 5.1 provides a typology.

Community care

Community work which is focused on the model of community care attempts to cultivate social networks and voluntary services for, or to be concerned about, the welfare of residents, particularly older people, persons with disabilities, and in many cases children under the age of five. The community care model concentrates on developing self-help concepts to address social and welfare needs and uses paid workers (sometimes termed 'organizers') who encourage people to care and to volunteer initiative. Professional involvement in community care can be on one of three levels. One level is where professionals are expected to fulfil a more or less permanent supportive or monitoring role, using volunteers and low-paid helpers. A second level is where the activity is initiated by professionals who plan to be supportive for only a short period, so that community care can be continued without them. A third level reflects community care as an activity undertaken by laypeople with relatively little help from professionals.

The voluntarism associated with the community care model supports the notion of engaging volunteers in care-giving (and advocacy schemes). In reality, there may be concerns over the level of training of volunteers and their reliability. Similarly, there may be concern about the exploitation of volunteers as free labour, which may also serve to undermine the jobs of paid workers.

In practice, the term 'informal care' refers to care undertaken by families, neighbours and friends, on an informal, unpaid basis and largely in the recipients' own homes. The important contribution of this sector has been recognized for some time. It has been estimated that the value of informal care ranges from £15 to £24 billion per year (Family Policy Studies Centre, 1989). Such calculations are very difficult to make with any accuracy as the defining feature of this sector is its informal and largely hidden nature. The figures were, however, arrived at using a notional rate of £4 per hour,

Table 5.1 Models of community work practice

	Strategy	Main role/title of worker	Examples of work/agencies	Selected critical key texts
Community care	Cultivating social networks and voluntary services Developing self-help concepts	Organizer Volunteer	Work with older people, persons with disabilities, children under 5 years	Beresford and Croft (1986) Heginbotham (1990) Mayo (1994)
Community organization	Improving co-ordination between different welfare agencies	Organizer Catalyst Manager	Councils for Voluntary Service Racial Equality Councils Settlements	Adamson et al. (1988) Dearlove (1974) Dominelli (1990)
Community development	Assisting groups to acquire the skills and confidence to improve quality of life Active participation	Enabler Neighbourhood worker Facilitator	Community groups Tenants groups Settlements	Association of Metropolitan Authorities (1993) Barr (1991)
Social/community planning	Analysis of social conditions, setting of goals and priorities, implementing and evaluating services and programmes	Enabler Facilitator	Localities undergoing redevelopment	Marris (1987) Twelvetrees (1991)
Community education	Attempts to bring education and community into a closer and more equal relationship	Educator Facilitator	Community schools/colleges 'Compensatory education' Working-class/feminist adult education	Allen et al. (1987) Allen and Martin (1992) Freire (1970; 1972; 1976; 1985) Lovett (1975) Lovett et al. (1983) Rogers (1994)

Table 5.1 cont'd

	Strategy	Main role/title of worker	Examples of work/agencies	Selected critical key texts
Community action	Usually class-based, conflict-focused direct action at local level	Activist	Squatting movement Welfare rights movement Resistance against planning and redevelopment Tenants' action	CDP literature (see Appendix A) Craig et al. (1982) Jacobs and Popple (1994) Lees and Mayo (1984)
Feminist community work	Improvement of women's welfare Working collectively to challenge and eradicate inequalities suffered by women	Activist Enabler Facilitator	Women's refuges Women's health groups Women's therapy centres	Barker (1986) Dixon et al. (1982) Dominelli (1990; 1994) Flynn et al. (1986)
Black and anti-racist community work	Setting up and running groups that support the needs of black people. Challenging racism	Activist Volunteer	Racial Equality Councils and Commission for Racial Equality funded projects	Ohri et al. (1982) Sivanandan (1976; 1990) Sondhi (1982; 1994)

irrespective of the level of care provided. This calculation takes no account of the additional expenditures (travel, adaptions, etc.) or of the opportunity costs in terms of careers and wages forgone by carers. Neither does it take any account of costs of childcare. The figure is useful, however, if only to offer an illustration of this sector's contribution in comparison to total government expenditure on social services in 1987–8 amounting to £3.34 billion (HM Treasury, 1987).

An optimistic view of the role of volunteers in community care is provided by Heginbotham (1990), who argues that a 'communitarian' approach to community care empowers people through their defining and participating in services for their own needs. He argues for a new vision of volunteering in which local services are managed by local people, an argument also persuasively made by Beresford and Croft (1986). Cutting across the arguments posited by different political groupings, Heginbotham (1990: 42) believes that there needs to be a balance between

> individual worth with collective responsibility, to fuse liberal economic ideals with market socialism, and to recognise the interplay between the central and the local state, on the one hand, and the community (often represented by voluntary organizations) on the other.

Heginbotham's laudable brave new world will attract few dissenters although his thesis has few practical examples of how it would work, and does not convincingly counter the criticism that a central tenet of the drive in the 1980s and 1990s towards community care can be viewed as minimizing state welfare expenditure (Walker, 1989).

Numerous studies have supported the view that women are much more likely to be engaged in community care than men (Croft, 1986; Equal Opportunities Commission, 1984; Finch and Groves, 1983; Lewis and Meredith, 1990; Ungerson, 1987). These findings are also reported by Parker (1981) who states that to talk about community or family care is to 'disguise reality':

> In fact, . . . 'care by the community' almost always means care by family members with little support from others in the 'community'. Further care by family members almost always means care by female members with little support from other relatives. It appears that 'shared care' is uncommon; once one person has been identified as the main carer other relatives withdraw.
>
> (Parker, 1981: 30)

Community care policies have been criticized by a number of social policy writers who point to the dominance of familist ideology, and its links with the wider ideology of possessive individualism (Dalley, 1988; Finch, 1984; Finch and Groves, 1985; Wicks, 1987). Dalley, for instance, argues that community care has been actively promoted by the Right for a number of reasons. These usually revolve around the need to avoid the expense of institutional care, but also because this form of care is perceived as the most 'appropriate' and 'natural' form of care for the dependent. This view is derived from the residualist or anti-collectivist approach to welfare whereby the family is seen as the locus of care, and the role of the statutory sector only comes into play when that unit has broken down in some way. The Barclay (1982), Griffiths (1988) and Wagner (1988) reports developed the policy and practice of community care models, endorsing the early development of localizing social work services that had been taking place in some areas (Hadley and Hatch, 1981; Hadley and McGrath, 1980), while hastening the development of community-based social work in local authorities elsewhere. The intention throughout was for social work departments to account more effectively for, and deliver, their services in the changing political, social and economic climate (Hadley et al., 1987).

Considerable discussion has been allocated here to the community care model. This is because during the late 1980s and the 1990s the model rapidly developed as a significant and relatively well-resourced form of community work which had clear connections with the ascendancy and influence of the New Right ideology of the same period (Leavitas, 1986; Loney et al., 1991). However, it needs to be noted that since the 1960s a number of social scientists have developed a critique of the failure of institutional care to provide people with humane treatment (Foucault, 1967; 1977; Goffman, 1961; Jones and Fowles, 1984; Morris, 1969; Robb, 1967; Scull, 1977; Townsend, 1962), while more recently the UK disability movement has stressed the desire of disabled people for independent living in mainstream housing rather than institutional care (Morris, 1990).

Community organization

Community work formulated on the community organization model has been used widely in Britain as a means of improving the co-ordination between different welfare agencies. Through such co-ordination it is thought possible to avoid duplication of services and poverty of resources while attempting to provide an efficient and effective delivery of welfare. Examples of community organizations are councils of voluntary service, older person's welfare committees, and 'similar organizations that are engaged in the co-ordination, promotion and development of the work of a number of bodies in a particular field at local, regional or national levels' (Jones, 1977: 6). The community organization model, which tends to be service-orientated, has been engaged in pioneering and experimental work and has often led to the state funding and managing the services developed by such organizations (Kramer, 1979).

Most critics of the community organization model underpin their arguments with theories from the radical and socialist approach. They include Dearlove (1974), who has cited the role of community organizations in employing 'expert' professionals whose job it is to offer advice to working-class people in an attempt to stifle the anger and frustration felt in a particular locality or community. The role of the 'expert' in this model is to channel these feelings into acceptable and approved structures. Dominelli (1990) takes up this point, arguing that community organization has been used by the local state in rationing its declining resource base. The Community Development Projects were also critical of the community organization model. They argued, for instance, that the Urban Deprivation Unit created by the Department of Environment in 1973 was based on the community organization model, operating with managerialist methods, and ignoring the needs and concerns of people living in the communities they professed to serve (CDP, 1977). Feminists have similarly criticized the community organization model (Dominelli, 1990: 10), although there has been evidence of feminists developing new styles of community organization (Adamson *et al.*, 1988).

Community development

The community development model of community work is concerned with assisting groups to acquire the skills and confidence to improve the quality of the lives of its members. With its emphasis on promoting self-help by means of education, this model is thought to reflect the 'uniqueness of community work' (Twelvetrees, 1991: 98). The community development model, which was championed in North America in the early 1960s by Biddle and Biddle (1965), evolved in Britain from the work initiated by Batten (1957; 1962; 1965; 1967) which, as observed in Chapter 3, initially derived from his experiences with such a model when working in the colonies. We also observed in Chapter 2 that this model of community work was used as a tool by British administrations overseas to harness the local communities into colonial domination. The rationale for the model being used by the British Colonial Office can be seen in HMSO (1954), while a similar notion is given in the United Nations statement on community development in developing countries (United Nations, 1959: 1). The use of the community development model in developing countries has been criticised by Ng (1988), who documents how the model was used in the colonies to integrate black people into subordinate positions within the dominant colonizing system.

The experience of community development in Britain has been characterized by work at the neighbourhood level and, as noted earlier, has focused upon a process whereby community groups are encouraged to articulate their problems and needs. The expectation is that this will lead to collective action in the determination and meeting of these needs. The typical worker in this model has been described by Dominelli (1990: 11) as 'usually a man who helps people learn by working on problems they have identified. He is typically a paid professional interested in reforming the system through social engineering'.

There are, of course, numerous examples of women being employed as community development workers. For example, a black woman, Anionwu (1990), has written up her community development work in relation to a marginalized health problem, sickle cell anaemia. Anionwu believes that the community development approach was successful in enabling her to meet and work with discriminated black sufferers, which led to her setting up the Brent Sickle Cell and Thalassic Centre.

Barr (1991) reviews and analyses Strathclyde Regional Council's programme of community development which is considered to be the most substantial of its kind in British local government. Discussion of his two field studies of the Social Work Department's community workers leads Barr to consider the role and practice of community development as a major policy initiative. In his findings Barr (1991: 166) argues that community development has a legitimate part to play in providing opportunities for 'radical alliances of professional, political and community interests to promote redistributive, anti-deprivation policies and practices'. Similarly, Roberts (1992) argues that community development workers based in local authority social services departments are in a position to contribute to the establishment and practice of imaginative community care proposals. He believes the skills and knowledge that are inherent in the community development model can be used to provide opportunities for people to achieve power and control over their own lives. This, he argues, will give community development a role within local government administration where the practice is under threat.

In his own work Barr draws the conclusion that community development workers would be more effective if they laid more emphasis upon social planning approaches. This was a concept established by Rothman (1976), who placed community development alongside social planning, and this has since been developed by Twelvetrees (1991). Twelvetrees (1991: 7) argues that whereas community development is involved in working alongside a particular community (whether locality or community of interest), social planning involves the community worker 'liaising and working directly with policy-makers and service providers to improve services or alter policies'. In some typologies of community work, and in particular those developed by Jones (1977), Rothman (1976), Thomas (1983) and Twelvetrees (1991), social planning is considered to be a discrete model of community work and it is to this area we now turn.

Social/community planning

As noted above, the social/community planning model of community work is considered to be similar to community development and has been described as

> the analysis of social conditions, social policies and agency services; the setting of goals and priorities; the design of service programmes and the mobilisation of appropriate resources; and the implementation and evaluation of services and programmes.
>
> (Thomas, 1983: 109)

The social/community planning model is believed to be the most common of community work models (Twelvetrees, 1991: 98). However, as Twelvetrees points out, this is complicated by the breadth of the term 'social/community planning', which can include economic planning and national planning. According to Twelvetrees, this means that although most community workers are engaged in social/community planning, not all those involved in this activity can be termed 'community workers'.

One of the advocates of social/community planning, which he calls simply 'community planning', is Marris (1987), who argues that it should be possible to incorporate the demand for open, democratic planning into political struggles for social justice. Marris believes that the failure of the Community Development Projects was due in part to their classical Marxist analysis of class relations which failed to recognize the subtle, complex and changing nature of working-class communities. He also believes that this focus on class antagonism led to an inability to work within the state to achieve improvements for the people who lived in the neighbourhoods the projects were intended to assist. Instead, Marris argues that if community work is to effect anything more than marginal change it needs to find common ground with the government even if the ideologies of the two are at variance. Marris suggests that social/community planning is one strategy that can be used to help protect working-class communities from the uncertainty and lack of control they suffer when redevelopment takes place in their locality. In Marris's view, then, community workers, including radical community workers, have more to gain for the communities they serve by developing a partnership with the state, and by practising the community planning model.

The main criticism that can be levelled at this view is that it assumes that the knowledge gained by community workers will be used by decision-makers in a rational manner for the benefit of the members of the community in question. Evidence from Marris is not entirely convincing. For example, he cites the redevelopment of London's docklands and the evolution of the Docklands Strategic Plan which attempted to involve and take account of the people living in the affected area (Newham Docklands Forum and Greater London Council Popular Planning Unit, 1983). He later admits, however, that the plan actually had little effect because

> plans are so often ignored, whenever they attempt to set priorities and guarantees in the interests of the most vulnerable, or constrain the freedom of action of those more powerful so as to reach some resolution which is both fair and practicable, [so that] planning even at its best often comes to seem merely a distraction from more effective forms of political protest, and so co-optive.
>
> (Marris, 1987: 160)

However, Marris continues to believe in the potential of the social/community planning model because political struggle without it leads only to 'competitive bargaining between different kinds of interests, and that cannot protect the weaker and more vulnerable members of society' (Marris, 1987: 160).

Community education

The community education model of community work has been described as 'a significant attempt to redirect educational policy and practice in ways which bring education and community into a closer and more equal relationship' (Allen *et al.*, 1987: 2). Community education has a long tradition in the United Kingdom which, according to I. Martin (1987), has evolved from three main strands. The first is the school-based village and community college movement initiated by Henry Morris in Cambridgeshire during the late 1920s (Morris, 1925). (For a discussion on the life and work of Morris see Rée, 1973; 1985.) This was followed by the establishment of similar integrated educational provision in Leicestershire under the guidance of Stewart Mason during the following decade (Fairbairn, 1979). The second strand of community education were the experiments developing from the Educational Priority Area projects (1969–72) which attempted to provide 'compensatory education' in selected disadvantaged inner-city areas as recommended by DES (1967). (For a detailed discussion of these experiments, see also Halsey, 1972; Midwinter, 1972; 1975.) The third strand was the working-class adult education work undertaken by a number of the Community Development Projects in the late 1960s and the early 1970s (for examples, see Lovett, 1975; Lovett *et al.*, 1983).

Community education has been further analysed as having three 'qualitatively different ideologies': consensus, pluralism, and conflict (I. Martin, 1987: 22). Martin argues that the consensus or universal model is focused around the secondary school/community college; the pluralist or reformist model is linked to primary schools and their neighbourhoods; and the conflict or radical model is focused around working-class action. To this can be added the feminist analysis of community education which is clearly articulated by Rogers (1994). The conflict or radical model shares with community development an emphasis on innovative, informal, political education, and has been greatly influenced by the Brazilian adult educator, Paulo Freire, whose work has served as a significant challenge to school-based education. It is because of his influence upon the practice of community work that we need to consider Freire's work in greater detail.

Working with poverty-stricken South American communities during the 1960s, Freire, who at the present time is resident professor of education at the University of São Paulo, Brazil, and visiting professor at Harvard's Centre for Studies in Education and Development, found ways of developing approaches by which people can express their feelings and experiences. He developed an educational process which rejects the traditional hierarchical 'banking system', where knowledge is considered to be a commodity accumulated in order to gain access to positions of power and privilege. In its place Freire developed an 'education for liberation' where learners and teachers engage in a process in which abstract and concrete knowledge, together with experience, are integrated into *praxis* (which can be defined as action intended to alter the material and social world). The fundamental features of this praxis are critical thinking and dialogue (as opposed to discussion) which seek to challenge conventional explanations of everyday life, while at the same time considering the action necessary for the transformation of oppressive conditions.

The extensive work of Freire (1970; 1972; 1976; 1985) centres on the concept of 'conscientization', otherwise known as politicization and political action. According to Freire, before people can engage in action for change they have first to reflect upon their present situation. However, the nature of ideological domination means that subordinate groups accept, and frequently collude with, the reproduction of a society's inequalities and the explanations and justifications offered for the status, power and privilege of their oppressors: an idea similar to notions developed by Gramsci. Overcoming this false ideology means overcoming people's pessimistic and fatalistic thinking. Freire understood this was not an easy task, but his great optimism and purpose have led to educators around the world taking up the challenge.

Freire believes that educators have to work on the wide range of experiences brought by oppressed people. The educational process entails providing opportunities for people to validate their experiences, culture, dreams, values and histories, while recognizing that such expressions carry both the seeds of radical change and the burden of oppression. Freire's position coincides with that held by many community workers that it is necessary to start from a person's own understanding. According to Freire, the skill is to work with people by a 'problematizing' approach rather than a 'problem-solving' stance as advocated in the banking system of education. 'Problem-solving' involves an expert being distant from a person's reality while engaging in an analysis that efficiently resolves difficulties before dictating a strategy of policy. Freire believes that this reduces human experience and difficulties to that which can be 'treated'. 'Problematizing', however, means immersing oneself in the struggle of disadvantaged communities and engaging in the task 'of codifying total reality into symbols which can generate critical consciousness' (Freire, 1976: ix).

According to Freire, this empowers people to begin to alter their social relations. Freire believes that this is undertaken by a process of critical reflection and action followed by further critical reflection and action. This, he continues, creates conditions for the development of genuine theory and collective action because both are rooted in a historical and cultural reality. However, Freire believes that theory and practice are not conflated into one another. Instead, there needs to be distance between the two. 'Theory does not dictate practice; rather, it serves to hold practice at arm's length in order to mediate and critically comprehend the type of praxis needed within a specific setting at a particular time in history' (Freire, 1985: xxiii).

Allman (1987) believes that Freire's ideas have begun to permeate liberal education in the United Kingdom but because of the structure and underlying ideology of the present system they are likely to be used only selectively. Similarly, Allman (1987: 214) argues that Freire's ideas have been distorted and devalued in the 'futile attempt to incorporate "radical" technique in the "liberal" agenda'. Taking note of these criticisms, Freire's work, together with the writings of Gramsci, has implications for the theory and practice of community work which we will consider in more detail in Chapter 7.

Community action

In our discussion in Chapter 2, we found that the community action model of community work was both a reaction to the more paternalistic forms of community work and a response by relatively powerless groups to increase their effectiveness. We have also discussed the way in which the Community Development Projects were initiated as a government-supported community work venture based upon the community organization and community development models. Soon after their commencement this direction changed, with the Projects evolving on the lines of the community action model.

The community action model of community work has traditionally been class-based and uses conflict and direct action, usually at a local level, in order to negotiate with power holders over what is often a single issue. Early writings on community action by, among others, Lapping (1970), Leonard (1975), Radford (1970) and Silburn (1971), together with the influential community work series of books published by Routledge & Kegan Paul in conjunction with the Association of Community Workers (Craig *et al.*, 1979; 1982; Curno, 1978; Jones and Mayo, 1975; Mayo, 1977; Mayo and Jones, 1974; Ohri *et al.*, 1982; Smith and Jones, 1981), as well as a number of other significant writings (for example Cockburn, 1977; Cowley *et al.*, 1977; Curno *et al.*, 1982; Lees and Mayo, 1984; O'Malley, 1977) provide a rich source of examples of the practice and debates surrounding the model during the late 1960s, 1970s and early 1980s. The North American community work literature also contains examples and discussions of community or social action. The texts that have been the most influential in the United Kingdom include Alinsky (1969; 1971); Lamoureux *et al.* (1989) and Piven and Cloward (1977).

Since the 1960s examples of community action have been varied and include the squatting movement, the welfare rights movement (including the Claimants Union), and different forms of resistance against planning and redevelopment. Mayo (1982) believes the most typical form of community action has focused around the issue of repairs and maintenance of council housing. This is reflected in the literature. The Association of Community Workers, for instance, devoted a publication to community work and tenant action (Henderson *et al.*, 1982), and considerable space was allocated to housing-related issues in the now defunct magazine *Community Action*.

An important strand of community action has been that linked with trade union activity (see, for example, Corkey and Craig, 1978; Craig *et al.*, 1979). This has often been as a direct result of the work of the Community Development Projects in a particular locality. Examples of the projects that arose from such an intervention include the Coventry Workshop, the Tyneside Trade Union Studies Unit, and the Joint Docklands Action Group. This type of action has been further developed in the 1980s and 1990s by municipal socialism, which has been based on a broad political group described as the 'new urban left'. Towards the end of the existence of the Greater London Council there were a plethora of supported community projects. However, Goodwin and Duncan (1986) argue that such policies are most effective in terms of political mobilization and that policy-makers on the left should be aware of the constraints and limitations of policies promising large-scale job creation and local economic regeneration. With rising unemployment, the issue of community action and the problems faced by people without employment became a concern during the early 1980s and have continued to be so to the present day (Cumella, 1984; Gallacher *et al.*, 1983; McMichael *et al.*, 1990; Ohri and Roberts, 1981; Purcell, 1982; Salmon, 1984), while community action and co-operatives have also been an important theme (*Roof*, 1986).

The role of the community worker in the community action model is an interesting one and highlights the tension within the state towards community work. We have noted in previous discussions that the majority of community work is sponsored by the state which, through its agencies, will define, supervise and regulate the work of practitioners. However, community action, by its very nature, is often engaged in conflict with the employers of community workers, the local authorities. A wider debate on the contradictions surrounding this position is addressed in *In and Against the State* (London Edinburgh Weekend Return Group, 1980). It is for this reason that community action is usually seen as an area of practice undertaken by campaigners and activists who are not employed, directly or indirectly, by the state. Thomas (1983) argues that one cannot conflate the role of community worker with that of community activist. They are, in his view, different, and clearly reflect his own adherence to the pluralist approach and practice theories.

> Community work interventions require a certain degree of experience and training; they offer specific skills and knowledge to a community or agency which are different from (though not inherently better than and often over lapping with) those offered by local residents who take on active roles within community groups.
>
> (Thomas, 1983: 11)

In the same book, which reviews the development of community work, Thomas does not discuss the role of community action other than in passing reference. Instead he focuses on community work as a specialist occupation, with 'a particular and limited intervention' (Thomas, 1983: 7), located in neighbourhoods and agencies. The decision by Thomas not to address the community action model highlights his view that community work is a profession, rather than a political activity.

Feminist community work

Chapter 3 outlined the evolution of feminist community work theory based on the development, since the 1960s, of feminist theory. Female community workers have applied these theoretical understandings to practice (see, for example, Dixon *et al.*, 1982), both in feminist campaigns and in permeating existing community work practice and principles (Dominelli, 1994; Dominelli and McLeod, 1989). While there is no agreed single theoretical feminist position, there is a consensus that the central aim of feminist community work practice is the improvement of women's welfare by collectively challenging the social determinants of women's inequality. Although much of the practice is focused at the personal, local or neighbourhood level, it is linked practically and theoretically with wider feminist concerns. For example, women have been active in many localities in providing accommodation, usually in the form of emergency housing, for battered women. This securement of safe accommodation is a response to the immediate suffering experienced by individual women at the hands of violent men, to the inadequate provision made by the state for such women, as well as presenting a stand against male violence (see, for example, Binney *et al.*, 1981; Hanmer and Maynard, 1987; Pahl, 1985a; Wilson, 1983).

Chapter 4 discussed the central role of the women's movement as a feature of new social movements, and how feminist campaigns are an example of practice that links local work with that undertaken at national level. As well as the example of local women's refuges, which are affiliated to the National Women's Aid Federation, we can note a number of other campaigns and networks which have both a local and a national profile. These include women's health groups (Roberts, 1982; Ruzek, 1986; Webb, 1986); women's involvement in the 1984–5 miners' strike (Bloomfield, 1986; Dolby, 1987; Lewycka, 1986; McCrindle and Rowbotham, 1986; Millar, 1987; Seddon, 1986; Waddington *et al.*, 1991; Whitham, 1986); the National Childcare Campaign, which, while influenced by the women's movement, included fathers, trade union members and social services workers (NCC, 1985); the Programme of the Reform on the Law of Soliciting (PROS), a Birmingham-based group of prostitutes whose aim was the abolition of prison sentences for loitering and soliciting (McLeod, 1982); the Wages for Housework grouping (Malos, 1980), the National Houseworking Group (Allen and Wolkowitz, 1986), and the Leicester Outwork Campaign (1987); abortion campaigns (Berer, 1988); campaigns highlighting the link between pornography and violence (Segal, 1990); Rape Crisis Centres (Pahl, 1985b); women's therapy centres (Doyal and Elston, 1986); Incest Survivor Groups (Armstrong, 1987; Dominelli, 1986; 1989; Kelly, 1988); the revolutionary feminist initiative Women Against Violence Against Women (McNeil and Rhodes, 1985); and the women's peace movement, in particular that focused on Greenham Common (Cook and Kirk, 1983; Feminism and Non-Violence Study Group, 1983; Finch, 1986; Harford and Hopkins, 1984). 'Women's issues' were also incorporated into developments in municipal socialism, but not without a degree of resistance from men (Cockburn, 1991).

As well as the commitment to working collectively to challenge and eradicate inequalities suffered by women, feminist community work practice emphasizes the objective of working with women's own personal experiences in groups. According to one influential writer in this area, this helps

redefine social problems and challenges the individualising and pathologising approaches to women's issues marking the practice of traditional community workers and social workers. Crucial to this challenge has been undoing the division of social problems into private matters requiring individual or family solutions and public issues in which a range of social forces including the state, formal agencies and the public intervened.

(Dominelli, 1990: 43)

This work is often undertaken in the form of consciousness-raising groups which were mentioned in our earlier discussion of feminist community work theory. Women's consciousness-raising groups are intended to break down feelings of isolation and provide participants with a sense of solidarity in order to engage in co-operative struggles. As we have seen above, consciousness-raising groups can also be used to provide women with the strength, knowledge and skill to challenge professionals' definition of their positions. Overall, these groups are considered by feminist community workers as an important first step in the process of change; it is a necessary but not sufficient condition for the transformation of social relations.

The use of women only groups, whether in specialist consciousness raising or in more general ways, is a central feature of feminist community work. Among its advocates, Hanmer and Statham (1988) argue that the quality of the group process is likely to be improved in a single-sex group, because the intimate and interpersonal problems are likely to be confronted more quickly. The authors claim that the realization that their problems are not unique should help to reduce women's feelings of personal inadequacy, and thus start to alleviate isolation and stigmatization. Similarly, research has shown that men take over and influence community groups by controlling the 'introduction and pursuit of topics, the use of available time, the lack of emotional content in conversation' (Hanmer and Statham, 1988: 131). This is confirmed by Gallacher (1977), who notes that men hold key positions in community associations.

Feminist community workers have engaged in a variety of creative attempts to develop non-hierarchical structures and more participatory ways of working. Criticisms of traditional forms of organization as being alienating and inaccessible initially resulted in attempts to develop structureless groups. However, there is a recognition that it is 'a mistake to equate structure with hierarchy' (Freeman, 1984: 62). This has led one writer to argue that 'the quest for a structure which is genuinely participatory, which does not alienate people, and yet achieves the goals which the group has set itself must be central to feminist practice within the women's movement and in community work' (Barker, 1986: 87).

Similarly, process models in group work have been of concern to feminist community workers who indicate that they can function to exclude and to intimidate group members. Process models are concerned with both the different stages a group moves through (for instance, reflection, planning and action) and the development individual group members achieve. According to Brown (1986), process models have two ideologically different positions. One emphasizes individual emotional growth and development. The other model is founded upon political and social philosophies and is engaged in achieving change for disadvantaged people. Previously the importance of process has been overlooked by radical community work because of the dominance of the former model. Dixon *et al.* (1982) argue, for instance, that this non-political approach was reflected in the writings of early theorists such as Batten. However, as they go on to state, 'Feminist analysis shows clearly that process is political, and needs urgent consideration if our campaigns are to achieve their aims' (Dixon *et al.*, 1982: 63).

The concern with regard to feminist community work is that the flow of written work in this area has been reduced to a trickle. The lack of recent feminist community work literature is commented upon by Dominelli (1990: 8), who highlights the fact that two of the main exponents of community work literature, David Thomas and Alan Twelvetrees, have 'virtually ignored the implications of gender'. Similarly, more radical texts appear to have included little on gender, something noted by Brandwein (1987) and Lee and Weeks (1991). When one considers the role women play in community work, whether as activists as described by Campbell (1993), or in administering a community work project as discussed by Brandwein (1987), it is clear that women have played a highly significant part in the practice. Dominelli (1990: 122) argues that women's contribution to community work has been undervalued. For instance, while there are texts that track the campaign work women have been engaged in (see Curno *et al.*, 1982; Mayo, 1977), the perception of women themselves has rarely been considered. The paucity of literature in this field indicates the need for further research and dissemination of results, if we are to increase our understanding in this important sphere of community work.

Black and anti-racist community work

Chapter 3 discussed how traditional forms of community work have failed both to meet the particular needs of the black community and to challenge institutional and personal racism. It also discussed the response to this by the black community and those community workers who are engaged in developing an anti-racist critique.

Historically there is evidence that the black community has not passively accepted racism and racist policy and practice. Since their arrival in Britain, black people have been active in their communities, supporting each other and organizing to resist discrimination and defend their rights (Bhat *et al.*, 1988; Hiro, 1992; Solomos, 1989). The focus of discrimination has varied, although frequently it has appeared as if black people have been and continue to be besieged in a number of areas including education, housing, immigration, health, employment, and police relations. Similarly, a range of different and overlapping responses has developed: campaigns; self-help groups; direct action; alternative and supplementary provision. At times these have required coalitions to be built and alliances forged, at others autonomous organization has been preferred. Unfortunately, for our purposes, few studies have been made of these community-based organizations and campaigns. At the time of writing, a detailed survey of the nature of black voluntary groups, their activities, sources and level of funding, composition and organization, is being undertaken by the Organization Development Unit of the National Council for Voluntary Organisations. Those studies that have been made tend to be limited in their scope (Solomos, 1989: 149). There is also evidence of black people being excluded from mainstream political life in Britain, which has led to migrants launching a number of local and national groupings including the Indian Workers' Association and the West Indian Standing Conference (Carter, 1986; Jacobs, 1986). Furthermore, Anwar (1986) argues that racial disadvantage and discrimination will only be solved when black people are included in the political process and in British public life.

The studies that have been made of the influence of black community-based organizations and groups provide useful insights. For instance, the work by Goulbourne (1987; 1990) indicates that certain autonomous black community-based groups have successfully influenced mainstream institutions by placing on the political agenda contentious issues, such as police relations with the black community and the education of black children. Cheetham (1988) meanwhile argues that ethnic associations in Britain have a vitality and energy that has assisted their development as active self-help groups. Kalka (1991) discusses the tension between entrenched local organizations and newly founded ethnic associations and pressure groups. The author describes the situation in the London Borough of Harrow where Gujarati Hindus became increasingly articulate in presenting demands and acquiring new skills to assert their position. Not all black groups have been able to gain effective representation and satisfactory resources. Bangladeshis are thought to be disadvantaged relative to other Asian communities in Britain (Carey and Shukur, 1985–86), while according to Fawzi El-Solh (1991) Somalis living in the Tower Hamlets area of London's East End, who rank as one of the oldest settled migrant groups in Britain's docklands, experience greater difficulties. Fawzi El-Solh argues that Somalis encounter obstacles to effective organization of their community, while their needs are not satisfactorily represented.

Other research that describes and discusses the role of, and work with, black community-based groups includes that by Sondhi (1982). Writing about his work at the Asian Resource Centre in the multi-racial community of Handsworth in Birmingham, Sondhi views the agency as a campaigning one that provides a much needed advice and information service in the locality. The agency also undertook specific work with the Asian elderly (Asian Sheltered Residential Accommodation, 1981). Mullard (1973) argues, however, that state-supported self-help groups channel the energy of black militants away from wider political struggles. This view is supported by James (1990), who believes that politically motivated and articulate black professionals suffer from a constant tension centred on the issue of whom they can best serve. In many cases such professionals have been absorbed into local authorities' hierarchies or into academic posts, and in the process have modified, or have been required to modify, their demands for improvements in the position of the black community. At the same time such workers retain their loyalty and commitment to their own community. This leads to black workers experiencing burnout, frustration and anger. On the one hand they are

> actively working with policy makers and colleagues to address the issues. On the other spending evenings and weekends with volunteers and community activists to help them articulate about the issues so that they may eventually work with the policy makers.
>
> (James, 1990: 32)

The establishment of community projects by the black population is often a response to exclusion from white-dominated provision as well as providing opportunities to develop and strengthen cultural, social and political ties. Although black people do not form a homogeneous group within Britain, they share with each other the experience of racism and of colonization which, as we noted earlier, has given them certain strengths and perspectives. Community work projects funded by the Commission for Racial Equality and Racial Equality Council have, however, met with criticism from two different sources. One argues that public funds should be given to projects that are for the whole community and not one particular group. This argument fails, however, to recognize structural racism, which leads to black people being excluded from mainstream organizations and the need for them to have separate provision. The other source of criticism has come from black radicals such as Sivanandan (1976; 1990), who believe that such projects dissolve and co-opt black protest. Within white-dominated community work the activity has only gradually addressed the issue of racism and it is felt in a number of quarters this has only been partial (Dominelli, 1990; Ohri et al., 1982). According to one writer, the central issue that needs to be addressed by white community workers is the continuing failure of institutions to provide equal treatment of black people while recognizing the specific needs of ethnic minorities (Loney, 1983: 54).

On a wider level, as noted in Chapter 2, since the passing of the 1948 British Nationality Act, and up to and since the 1988 Immigration Act, 'race' and immigration have been central issues in British political life. During the early 1980s a number of mainly Labour-controlled local authorities attempted to operate and implement racial equality policies and practices. In at least one study these were to prove that the local political scene was an important site of struggle, particularly for local organizations committed to racial equality (Ben-Tovim et al., 1986). The abolition of the Greater London Council in March 1986 was believed to have serious implications for black residents of the capital since it left no city-wide commitment to support the black community and no agreement to tackle racism (Adeyemi, 1985). There has been some criticism by black writers that well-intentioned white people incorporated the black struggle in the local authority anti-racist strategies of this period (see, for example, Bhavnani, 1986; Gilroy, 1987). These writers and others (Mullard, 1984; Troyna, 1987; Troyna and Carrington, 1990) criticize multi-cultural education strategies which emphasize cultural pluralism and

equality in a setting of economic and social inequality. With these limitations recognized, it is important not to overlook the contribution from white
anti-racists in community work to the struggle for equal opportunities and
for the provision of more resources for the black community, and in 'con-
front[ing] racism, sexism and other forms of discrimination both within
ourselves and within society' (Association of Community Workers, 1982).

An example of community workers with an anti-racist approach successfully confronting racism and harassment is offered by Buckingham and Martin
(1989). Working in and around a north London housing estate, the workers
describe and reflect on their use of community development principles and
practice to reduce the harassment endured by the Bangladeshis living in
the area. A further example is a training aid for confronting anti-racism in
the form of a video that has been produced by Rooney Martin (1987). The
video shows a group of white people from a variety of backgrounds including English, Irish, Jewish and working-class, discussing what it means to be
white from their particular standpoint. The main function of the video is to
sensitize white people to the need to understand whiteness and how their
colour affects their culture and their relationships with non-white people.

The national Commission for Racial Equality and local Racial Equality Councils have been active in supporting black and anti-racist community work.
The national survey by Francis et al. (1984: 11) found that 72% of all Community Relations Councils' community workers came from black groups,
and whereas 59% of all community workers were employed in the voluntary
sector, 81% of black community workers were employed in this sector. There
have been certain criticisms, however, that the black community should not
have to rely on government-sponsored bodies or the voluntary sector, but
rather they need to be able to deal directly with their local authorities and
elected representatives. John (1981) argues, for instance, that black workers
should be employed by local authorities rather than by a vulnerable, often
unaccountable voluntary sector which serves to place the needs of the black
community at the margins of social and political life.

Finally, Ohri et al. (1982) argue that the primary issue for the black community and the one which community work must address if it is to remain
relevant to the needs and concerns of black people, is the resistance to
racism.

Conclusion

In conclusion, we can see that although there is overlap between the models
discussed, particularly in terms of techniques and skills used, the models
reflect the different traditions and ideologies that we have been alerted to
in previous chapters. Community care, community organization, community development and social/community planning represent the pluralist tradition in community work. The community action model and the emerging
models from feminism and the black and anti-racist critique reflect a radical
and socialist approach. Different aspects of community education fit into

different approaches. The radical strand of the model is epitomized in the work of Freire and of Lovett. The work of school-based community education, including the compensatory education programmes, is, however, an example of the pluralist approach. Certain models, for instance community care and social/community planning, are centred upon the premise of delivering a service in a more efficient and often cost-effective or cost-saving manner. Other models, such as those from the radical and socialist approaches, are focused around certain ideological positions and commitments. Together with the remaining models the above offers us a framework in which to understand community work practice.

One important question that emerges from the discussion on the theories of community work and the above discussion on models, is whether all those employed as community workers in organizations practising the pluralist models are in total agreement with the aspirations offered by such models. For instance socialist feminists, who have a particular view of society and on how it should be organized, may be employed in community care, pluralist community education, community development or other community work positions. Traditionally workers in these areas are required to act in a 'neutral' manner and to develop formal links with policy-makers in order to improve services for a particular community in a manner which endorses the status quo. We will return to the question of whether these models, with their particular style, hinder or assist in the achievement of workers' ideological aspirations in the final chapter.

Chapter **6**

COMMUNITY WORK IN PRACTICE

Introduction

Chapter 5 considered in detail the range of different community work models that reflect the nature and breadth of the activity. We noted that these models provide us with an important method of relating the theoretical discussions generated in Chapters 3 and 4 with various forms of community work practice. Together these three chapters have provided us with a detailed account and a clearer understanding of significant constituent elements of community work theory and practice.

The purpose of this chapter is to link this developing discussion with a number of central practice themes that have been generated at various stages in this book but which we have not been able to discuss in detail. The literature on the development of community work, and that relating to the theory of community work and the differing models, have revealed themes that are central to community work practice. We have seen, for example, in our discussion on the development of community work that recruitment, training, employment and funding have been central, yet changing themes in the evolution of the practice. Furthermore, personal experience as a practitioner, and now as an educator, has alerted me to the importance of these debates within community work. In our consideration of contemporary community work we need, therefore, to examine these areas in more depth. Skills are also a salient feature of practice, and we have noted the emphasis attributed to them in the pluralist approach. Finally, we need to consider in more detail the management of community work, to which hitherto we have made only passing reference. The chapter develops these themes in sequence: recruitment; training; employment and funding; skills; and the management of community work.

Recruitment

One of the main features of community work recruitment is that it is an 'open occupation', which, according to Smith (1980), gives it a degree of richness, vitality and variety. Likewise, Thomas (1983: 185) argues for the necessity of an 'open occupation' philosophy and policy in order to encourage people from a range of backgrounds to take up community work. Thomas provides a caveat stating that the policy needs to be set alongside adequate training opportunities and the establishment of a national qualification in community work.

Unfortunately there is little hard evidence on the recruitment of community workers. The most comprehensive research was undertaken by Francis *et al.* (1984), whose survey of community workers in the United Kingdom is now over ten years old. This postal survey counted 5,365 full- or part-time community workers on contracts of 12 months or more. The data from two smaller but more recent surveys are also included here. One is a survey of 232 community workers in the United Kingdom undertaken in 1990 (Convention of Scottish Local Authorities, 1990). The other is a survey of 246 community practitioners in Bradford undertaken in 1992 (Glenn, 1993). In the Francis *et al.* survey nearly half of all community workers surveyed were women, while in the more recent surveys the figures reflect the employment of more women (see Table 6.1).

In the Francis *et al.* survey, 13% of respondents might be termed to be from 'ethnic/national minorities', most of whom were represented as follows:

(i)   those working in London (27% of the 788 London workers were from a minority ethnic group);
(ii) those working in Community Relations Councils (72% of 156);
(iii) those funded by the Commission for Racial Equality (62% of 189).

The recent survey by the Convention of Scottish Local Authorities shows a much smaller percentage of community workers from an ethnic group

Table 6.1 Community workers by gender

	Male (%)	Female (%)	Number of respondents
Francis *et al.* (1984)	53	47	3,852
Convention of Scottish Local Authorities (1990)	47	53	232
Glenn (1993)*	37	61	231

*The gender of 2% of workers was unknown.

Table 6.2 Percentage distribution of community workers by age

Francis et al. (1984)		Glenn (1993)	
Under 25	11	Under 25	<3
25–29	24	25–29	12
30–34	23	30–39	41
35–39	16	40–49	34
40–44	10	50–64	9
45–64	16	65+	–
65+	<0.5	Did not say	<1
Number of respondents	3,831		231

(6%). The Bradford survey highlights the fact that 21% of its respondents were from either an Indian, Pakistani, Bangladeshi, Other Asian or Afro-Caribbean background.

The research by Francis et al. reveals that over one-third (35%) of community workers are less than 30 years old, whereas the work by Glenn shows that only 15% are under the age of 30 years while most were drawn from the 30–50 age group (see Table 6.2). Francis et al.'s (1984: 12) research discovered that 51% of respondents held a degree, or near equivalent, making them 'much more highly educated than the population as a whole'. In the 1984 and 1993 surveys those who possessed a training qualification were less prevalent than degree holders, a point to which we will return in the section on training. For example, in the Bradford survey 57% of respondents indicated they had one or more professional qualifications. The figures were: qualifications in Youth and Community work, 21%; teaching, 15%; social work, 9%; management, 5%; nursing, 2% and health education/promotion, 2%. From all three surveys we can observe a general profile of recruits to community work in which the practitioners are, on the whole, well educated and white, with more women than men undertaking the work.

Jeffs and Smith (1990) quote the work of Lowe (1973), who found that 22% of full-time youth and community workers came from skilled manual or related trades. A decade later, Kuper (1985) had found that the situation with regard to full-time youth and community workers had changed. Using data collected in 1983, she discovered that 43% were qualified teachers, 27% had undertaken specialist training, 17% had received training by alternative routes or had gained individual recognition, and 13% were unqualified. Figures from Holmes (1988), which are not entirely comparable, indicate that 36% of youth and community workers were previously trained as teachers, while 37% had received specialist training. The data from both sources do not include details on the workers' class background.

From 1977 until the early 1990s the 13 community and youth work training agencies providing full-time training conducted an annual enquiry into their recruitment (Parr, 1991). Unfortunately it was not until 1983 that the questionnaire was enlarged to provide details of gender and ethnic origins. However, for the eight-year period from 1983 to 1991 26% of the actual intake of the two-year course were from minority ethnic backgrounds. The figure for the same period for the one-year postgraduate courses was 8.4%, reflecting the educational discrimination experienced by black people (Carr-Hill and Chadha-Boreham, 1988). The ratio of females to males on the two-year courses for the period was 50.2% to 49.8%. On the one-year courses women out numbered men by 8.6% (45.7% male, 54.3% female).

One of the training agencies, Westhill College in Birmingham, was able to provide me with more up-to-date details of their two full-time training courses. On the two-year course the ratio of females to males was 60% to 40% for the 1993 and 1994 intakes, with a 50/50 balance on the one-year course. In the 1993 entry students from ethnic minorities were in the majority, but in 1994 they formed only one-third of the two-year course intake. The head of department at the College suggests this may be due to the move to UCAS (University Clearing and Admissions System). A third of students on the one-year course are from ethnic minority groups (Holmes, personal communication, 16 November 1994).

Although we do not possess up-to-date or exact data relating specifically to community work, we can note certain recruitment trends. One is the growth in the number of women in post, so that there appear to be more females in employment than males. These figures do not account for those in unpaid posts, and we can only speculate that women will be well represented in these positions. We have also noted the percentage of black workers entering the field. We are on less certain ground when we consider age, although the surveys are indicating that recruits to the practice tend to be around 30 years of age. We also note that community workers have usually gained a degree and/or a professional qualification.

Training

Community work training can be divided into college-based and field-based training. Historically, there has always been an element within the community work occupation that is ambivalent, and at times antagonistic, towards college-based training courses. In recent years there has been a move to overcome these differences and in 1990 a working group, titled the Community Work Forum of Interest and involving a number of interested groups (representatives of the regional training boards; the Association of Community Workers; the Federation of Community Work Training Groups; the National Federation of Community Organisations; the Community and Youth Work Union; the Federation of Black Community Workers and Trainers; the European Federation of Black Community Organisations; and the British Association of Settlements and Social Action Centres), was convened by the Federation of Community Work Training Groups in an attempt to develop a practice-based route. There was concern that college-based youth and community work courses were having to move towards youth work, while the Forum of Interest was concerned with working towards nationally recognized awards in community work. Its proposals are the first to come from an influential grouping representing the practice of community work (Federation of Community Work Training Groups, 1991).

The issue addressed by these proposals was to provide a co-ordinated and agreed standard of appropriate training for the diverse range of people who undertake or wish to undertake community work. This, the working group argues, demands an equally diverse range of accessible training opportunities.

A major concern for the Community Work Forum of Interest was the lack of a nationally recognized community work award. At present four different routes can be taken to becoming qualified in community work. However, there is a lack of commonality between the various routes, with a diversity of material taught, and different bodies validating the awards, none of which has community work as its main or only focus. One of the qualifying routes is through college-based training, and there are three routes through field-based training. We now discuss these.

College-based training

College-based community work training takes place in a range of full-time courses at post-graduate, post-qualifying, and initial training levels which include community work theory and practice as a constituent part of a wider study base. In recent years college-based training has been broadened to include a small number of part-time courses. These certificates and diplomas, such as the Diploma in Social Work and the Diploma in Youth and Community Work, are awarded by various bodies. A recent study indicates that the majority of trained community workers are graduates of these youth and community work courses (Convention of Scottish Local Authorities, 1990). As well as the sub-degree routes community workers are trained through first degree courses. For social work the validating body is the Central Council for Education and Training in Social Work (CCETSW). Youth and community work certificates and diplomas are awarded by universities, and if they have an appropriate and substantial youth work content they are endorsed by the National Youth Agency and recognized by the Joint Negotiating Council for Youth and Community Work. In Scotland community workers have to be graduates in order to obtain paid employment in their field.

Although a general feature of college-based social work and youth and community work courses has been a slow erosion of the community work content (Federation of Community Work Training Groups, 1992), there is evidence that community work theory and practice are being taught on a number of courses in higher education. So, although the CCETSW disbanded its Community Work Interest Group in 1991 (Association of Community Workers, 1991), a small number of the recently validated Diploma in Social Work courses have indicated that community work is offered as an area of particular practice. This is in addition to the CCETSW-approved post-qualifying MA in Social and Community Work Studies which is offered at the University of Bradford. The demise of the Council for Education and Training in Youth and Community Work and its absorption into the National Youth Agency has led to community work training being resourced only as part of youth work training.

As we noted in Chapter 2 when we discussed the development of community work, the activity has been associated with youth work since the late 1960s. It was in the aftermath of the Fairbairn-Milson Report (DES, 1969) that existing youth work training courses retitled themselves 'youth and community work' training courses (Jeffs, 1979: 61). This 'set youth work within the context of community development and its contribution towards a more participatory democracy' (Thomas, 1983: 27).

The Conservative governments of the 1980s and 1990s, through the Department of Education and Science (later the Department for Education), were keen to emphasize youth work at the expense of community work both on training courses and in the delivery of local authority youth services. This was because many of the traditional youth work posts that related to the management and administration of purpose-built youth clubs were difficult to fill. Instead, many graduates from youth and community work courses preferred employment in community work rather than youth work, or chose to work in other 'people-work professions' such as social work (Kuper, 1985). The move to youth work rather than youth and community work was also influenced by the government's belief that youth workers had a role in providing activities and support to unemployed young people (Spence, 1985; Williamson, 1988).

Field-based training

There are three main forms of field-based training, all of which are relatively recent developments. They are: apprenticeship schemes; accreditation schemes; and courses offering introductory skills and reflective practice. Since 1985, there have been a number of pilot projects to develop courses or programmes to follow on from short introductory courses in community work. These were formerly called Stage 2 courses but are now often referred to as community work learning programmes to recognize and emphasize the individually negotiated learning element of the work. In future, these programmes are likely to be at Certificate in Higher Education level.

Apprenticeship is a programme of training which emphasizes 'learning and doing', with apprentices undertaking supervised employment. The criteria for a person being accepted on to a scheme rest with their suitable previous experience and not their academic qualifications. Although apprenticeship schemes can use college resources and tutors, the emphasis is on the individual and group learning needs. Apprenticeship schemes tend to be more closely linked with youth work than community work and are aimed particularly at local authority employees rather than those active in the voluntary sector. Perhaps the most established of the youth and community work apprenticeship schemes is Turning Point in south east London, where apprentices spend part of their week in an agency and the remainder of the time attending seminars and undertaking structured study (Sinclair, 1987). As part of the government's response to the needs of inner-city young people, the Department of Education and Science announced an expansion of the Youth and Community Work Apprenticeship Scheme between 1989 and 1993 involving the investment of approximately £12 million in 25 local authorities in 17 locations (D. Scott, 1990: 17).

Accreditation schemes, on the other hand, are not strictly a training mode, rather a method by which an assessment can be made of whether a person's previous community work experience is appropriate and whether the person is competent enough to warrant being recommended for a community work appointment. Accreditation is available to paid and unpaid community workers with a minimum of three years' full-time experience, or the equivalent in part-time or voluntary sessions. As with apprenticeship schemes, previous academic background is considered less important than work experience. In most cases a candidate creates a 'portfolio' of work to demonstrate having learnt from her/his experiences, and to confirm that the learning is relevant to occupational competences. There is no agreed format for this but it can include certificates, testimonies, photographs, drawings, cuttings and written work (D. Scott, 1990: 162). The idea of portfolios in the youth and community work field evolved from the work of Redman and Rogers (1984) and Bolger and Scott (1984). The Federation of Community Work Training Groups has been at the forefront in the development of accreditation schemes as a means of substantiating and validating the experiences of unqualified working-class women and men who have been involved in community work (Sapin, 1989). Successful applicants are awarded a National Youth Agency endorsed Certificate in Youth and Community Work if they have practised for the minimum period and can produce the required portfolio of work (Federation of Community Work Training Groups, 1991).

Courses provided by regional groups of the Federation of Community Work Training Groups, local authorities and further education college access programmes, and offering introductory skills and reflective practice, have been developed in certain parts of Britain. These courses are part-time and intended for those engaged in community work practice, and most are validated by the Open College network. At the time of writing, there are a number of basic courses of this kind in different parts of Britain.

At a wider level a significant change has taken place in the way vocational qualifications are offered and validated. The White Paper on vocational qualifications (HMSO, 1986) highlighted the inadequate investment available for training, and it recognized vocational skills and proposed new methods of assessing these. As a result the government set up the National Council for Vocational Qualifications to develop a structure and framework for recognizing workers' knowledge, skills, experience and qualifications in all areas of the economy, including the professions such as accountancy and law. In Scotland, the Scottish Vocational Education Council (SCOTVEC) was established and devised the Scottish Vocational Qualifications (SVQs). In England, Wales and Northern Ireland the new qualifications were titled National Vocational

Qualifications (NVQs). In all aspects the SQVs and NVQs are similar and are usually referred to as S/NVQs. According to Jessup (1990: 17), the framework was to rationalize the 'qualification jungle' which led to 'numerous awarding bodies competing in the same or overlapping occupational areas, with qualifications with different objectives, size and structure, often with no procedures for recognizing each [other's] qualifications.'

Since 1988 the National Council for Vocational Qualifications, through the Care Sector Consortium, which covers health, personal social services and the criminal justice services, has endorsed more than 1 million care workers with National Vocational Qualifications (Central Council for Education and Training in Social Work, 1992). Endorsement does not rely on a worker's training but on work-related standards of 'competence' designed to demonstrate knowledge and skills.

In 1990 the Department of Employment commissioned a feasibility study to see if it was possible to develop S/NVQs for community work. The results of the research indicated a positive response and the Federation of Community Work Training Groups has worked together with the Department of Employment, the National Council for Vocational Qualifications and the Scottish Vocational Education Council to formulate standards which will lead to S/NVQs based upon them. In the meantime the Federation of Community Work Training Groups Forum of Interest held a National Conference in November 1994 at which it was agreed to consider establishing a transnational standards body across Scotland, Wales, Northern Ireland and England, to develop and maintain national standards in community work and establish a lead body for this work. At the same time an interim board for England is to be established; the Scottish board may well come from an existing board, and in Northern Ireland and Wales meetings are planned to consider developments. This is an exciting innovation which will lead eventually to clearer and more co-ordinated procedures for developing and endorsing community work training and qualifications.

Diversity of training: a strength and a weakness

It can be seen from this discussion on both college-based and field-based training that the diverse nature of community work training is both its strength and its weakness. Its strength would appear to be the different routes and often innovative ways in which training is offered to a range of practitioners. The advantage of such training is that it can respond to the changing demands and needs of students and the field. It also means that community activists who would not entertain the idea of enrolling for a college-based course, or cannot attend a course because of care or family responsibilities, because of lack of financial resources to take a full- or part-time course, or because there are no relevant local opportunities for training, do have the opportunity to undertake training in ways more appropriate to their experiences and learning needs. The weakness has to be the patchy nature of provision and the reluctance of some employers to accept that certain qualifications are appropriate for community work posts. Hence the

Community Work Forum of Interest has proposed that all training routes 'should have equal value and status and be recognized nationally' (Federation of Community Work Training Groups, 1992: 5). To this end there is pressure to harness the four existing modes of training to produce a nationally recognized qualification in community work in 'its own right' (Federation of Community Work Training Groups, 1992: 2).

However, the number of community workers in post who have undertaken training appears small. Although we do not possess reliable, up-to-date statistics on the number of qualified community workers, the Community Work Feasibility Study indicated that the number of full- and part-time community workers who would be interested in acquiring a community work qualification could total several thousand (Convention of Scottish Local Authorities, 1990: 6).

One of the concerns raised in relation to the changing nature of training of community workers is the ascendancy of training over education (Issitt and Woodward, 1992: 43). Critics point to a contradiction in the training of community workers. On the one hand, there is a top-down state policy of restructuring education and training to ensure they become less person-centred and more performance-orientated in order more clearly to serve the needs of the market. This could mean jettisoning some of the central tenets of liberal adult education which would only be funded if it can be shown to have a vocational focus. On the other hand, there has been, as we have noted above, a bottom-up policy that emphasizes the differing and alternative routes to qualification which start with the needs of the student. As Issitt and Woodward (1992: 45) point out, this reveals a contradiction in the 'post-Thatcher 1990's', for it 'is not collective but individualistic solutions that are sought, through "active citizens" who find their own routes to the competence required by employers, enabling them to work and provide for themselves'. In 1994 a conference called to consider the Stage 2 developments made reference to this concern and had endorsed the proposal that collective approaches to learning would form the core of any community work programme at this level.

A further concern that needs to be raised in the changing nature of training for community work is the way in which terminology is used in relation to assessing competences of workers. As Pye (1991) has argued, the National Council for Vocational Qualifications is employing an academic tradition that emphasizes the behaviourist and positivist explanations of human actions. Stanley and Wise (1983: 108) point out that this position assumes that it is possible to measure and to explain human action and social reality in a scientific manner. These explanations argue that people's behaviour can in some way be objectified and assessed. The outcome of this has been the creation of check-list assessment in person-centred employment where students are required to meet certain competences; this can over-simplify the complexity of working with people, where it is necessary for good practice to acknowledge the holistic nature of social phenomena (Birke, 1986: 57).

As we have noted throughout our discussion on the theory and practice of community work, a central theme has been that the activity is concerned with working with and for the poor and disadvantaged in society. In recent years this has been reflected in the development of anti-discriminatory practice which has become a requirement of courses seeking professional endorsement (Council for Education and Training in Youth and Community Work, 1989: 5). The issue now will be how far the newly developed competences being suggested by the National Council for Vocational Qualifications will be able to accommodate these values and how they will be assessed. This is, of course, an issue for all the practice routes to qualification in community work.

Employment and funding

Now that we have an understanding of the recruitment pattern of practitioners together with the different routes they can take to obtain qualifications, it is appropriate to continue by examining the employment of community workers and the funding of the practice.

One of the main features of the employment of community workers is the variety of job titles given to people practising in what we have discovered is a broad area of work. Francis et al. (1984: 15) provide a definition of community work that includes the following job designations: neighbourhood advice workers; housing advice centre community workers; community initiatives officers; economic development workers; social development officers; community work assistants; and community youth workers. The Convention of Scottish Local Authorities (1990: 7) has a broader interpretation of the activity and list 33 job categories that it believes would find its proposed community work training units of relevance (see Appendix B).

It is this diverse and seemingly expanding list of job titles that points to the issue, discussed previously, that the terms community and community work are 'catch-all' terms that cover a multitude of meanings and activity. However, it needs to be recognized that a number of occupations have incorporated and adapted community work techniques, although very few allow their workers to be engaged in community work full-time. (For further discussion on the effect of this 'permeation' of community work practice into other work, see Butcher, 1986; Cliffe, 1985; Munday, 1980; Thomas, 1983.) It is helpful, therefore, to remind ourselves that we are using as a working definition of community work that offered by Taylor and Presley (1987: 2) and set out earlier on page 5.

As we noted in Chapter 2 in the discussion on the development of community work, there are two main strands to the funding of the activity. One is the public sector, through central and local government; the other through voluntary and charitable organizations. Butcher (1992: 146) provides a helpful diagram (Figure 6.1) to illustrate, in a generalized form, the diversity of community work appointments, and suggests the types of posts and roles that can be found in the two sectors.

Although the state, and in particular local authorities, were heavily involved in the employment of community workers in the 1970s, by the time

Figure 6.1 Community work: sponsorship and employment

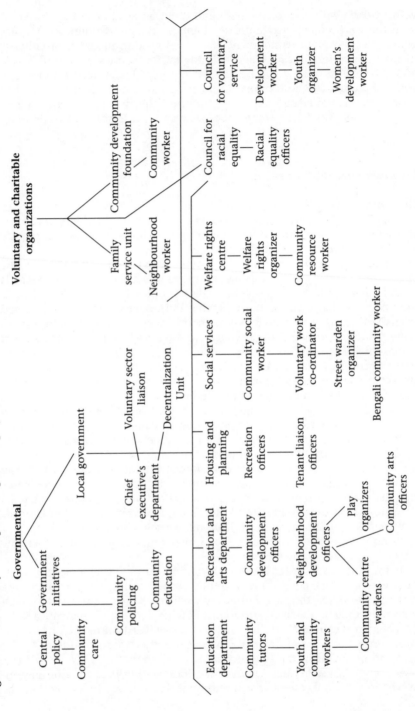

Source: Butcher (1992: 146)

Francis *et al.* (1984) carried out their survey of community workers, 59% of practitioners were still employed in the voluntary sector, with 85% of the funding in the voluntary sector coming from statutory sources (Francis *et al.*, 1984: 6). The question we need to ask is whether there has been any great change in this situation. Butcher (1992: 150) thinks there is no evidence to suggest that the proportion employed by voluntary organizations has changed, although 'questions must be raised as to whether the funding base has not changed quite rapidly'.

One of the central features regarding the employment and funding of community work that has been recurrent in its development, and continues at the present time, is the variety of usually short-term sources to fund community work and employ its practitioners. The unstable funding of projects and the employment of practitioners has persistently led observers to consider community work as experimental, with 'quite a high turn over of practitioners with little job security' (McConnell, 1992: 109), or to view it as the 'tyranny of the short-term' (Thomas 1983: 238). However, there has been one constant target for these different short-term sources of community work funding, that of inner-city areas, and it is such areas that we need to consider in more detail. Similar to other areas of government policy, the policies adopted for the inner city since the Conservatives came to power have reflected the free market approach and the shift away from government intervention (Hampton, 1991). Central government has placed severe financial restraints on local government spending and on the Urban Aid Programme, and promoted a batch of new programmes, initiatives and schemes aimed at economically regenerating inner-city areas. These programmes are set out in Figure 6.2.

We can see from Figure 6.2 that during the 1980s six central government departments were responsible for over 30 inner-city initiatives and programmes designated under the heading of Action for Cities. The central department dealing with inner-city policy has been the Department of Environment which has had within its responsibility a number of strategic programmes that focus upon the inner cities. Although expenditure on the inner cities has risen since 1979–80, the amount devoted to the Urban Programme has steadily dropped both in real and actual terms since 1982–3. It has been estimated that the Urban Programme, which was spending £280 million in 1990, will be allocated only £71 million in 1996. This has been in sharp contrast to the rise in money allocated to the economic regeneration programme which has included the Urban Development Corporation programme, grants for urban development, and expenditure on the Enterprise Zones which were established in 1981. However, recent figures indicate that there is to be a substantial drop in support for the Urban Development Corporations, with their spending reducing from £754 million in 1990–91 to £255 million in 1995–6.

Although the response to the inner city remains piecemeal and fails to tackle the fundamental problems facing residents living in inner-city areas (National Council for Voluntary Organisations, 1988), the effect on community work funding has been significant. The Urban Programme, which is the

Figure 6.2 Inner-city policy in the 1980s

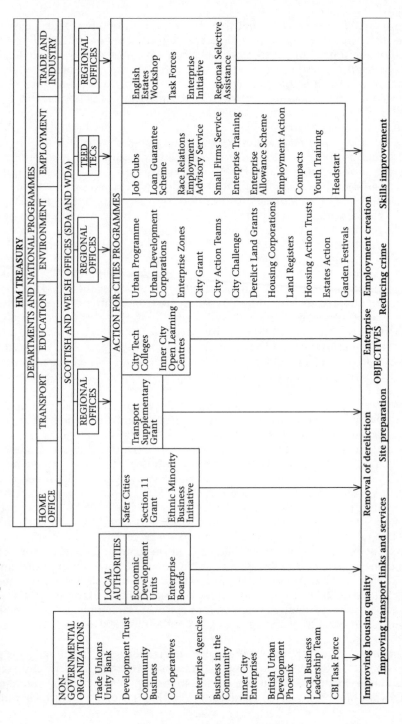

Source: Moore (1992: 124)

main conduit of central government money for community work and is co-ordinated and administered by local authorities, has four main objectives: to reduce derelict sites; to improve employment prospects; to strengthen the social fabric and encourage self-help; and to reduce the number of people in acute housing stress. According to Moore (1992: 130), 'almost three quarters of expenditure is on economic and environmental projects with the remainder on social and housing projects'. This means that in the year 1990–91 approximately £61 million of the yearly Urban Programme was allocated to social and housing projects. The Department of Environment has used nine broad headings to classify these projects, as follows: education; personal social services; advice and information services; housing; crime prevention; sport; recreation and leisure; play; and health (Whitting et al., 1986: 26). Descriptions of a selection of case studies by Whitting et al. (1986: 26–35) reflect the breadth of projects supported by the Urban Programme. The projects evaluated by Whitting et al. are those for the young unemployed. Community work is also funded through non-governmental organizations which receive funding from central and local government (see Figure 6.2).

A later development of central government funding for community work in inner-city areas has been the Department of Environment's City Challenge, launched in 1991. Local authorities compete with each other for money from City Challenge. Those that are successful each receive £37.5 million paid over 5 years. The initiative, which requires bids from partnerships of local authorities, the community and the private sector at local level, has been dismissed by critics as a 'lottery' (Hetherington, 1992) and 'a cynical political gesture – there is no new money, and it is neatly timed to coincide with a major financial squeeze on local government' (Green, 1992: 175).

A major funder of community work in the capital city is the London Borough Grants Committee which took over the London-wide and cross-borough funding after the abolition of the Greater London Council in 1986. The budget allocated to the 650 groups they fund was £29 million in 1991–2, a reduction of £4 million in real terms on the previous financial year. There is evidence that central government influenced the setting of this lower budget through the then Local Government Minister, Michael Portillo (Association of Researchers in Voluntary Action and Community Involvement, 1991). In Britain as a whole local authorities contributed almost £520 million to voluntary organizations during 1989–90. Approximately 51% of this total came from metropolitan authorities; 36% from county councils; and 13% from district councils. Voluntary organizations reported difficulties in obtaining funding from local authorities during the previous two financial years, 1987–9; central government had 'effectively capped many of its own funding programmes, and is in the process of reviewing its objectives for funding voluntary organisations' (Association of Researchers in Voluntary Action and Community Involvement, 1992: 12).

Voluntary groups working with ethnic groups have been particularly badly hit in recent years. A report commissioned by the Urban Trust and based on a survey of 111 ethnic minority groups and 102 trusts and corporate donors, found that 29% of the groups reported a cut in their local authority grant and 53% a cut in statutory funding. Although 16% reported a rise in their local authority grant and 25% a rise in statutory funding, the net effect has been a loss of state support which was the main income for 71% of the groups (Directory of Social Change, 1992).

As indicated in Chapter 2, the future of the Urban Programme is problematic. In November 1992, the government announced the reduction and eventual withdrawal of the Urban Programme. The City Challenge programme will not be continued after the allocation of the second round of bids. In place of the Urban Programme the government is establishing the Capital Partnership Programme and an Urban Partnership Fund. The Capital Partnership Programme will receive £200 million from different budget sources (not new money) to finance housing, environmental and urban schemes. The Urban Partnership Fund element of this is £20 million, compared with £237.1 million spent on the Urban Programme in 1992–3. The voluntary sector is largely excluded from the Urban Partnership Fund as a result of a restriction on money to be spent on capital projects. The reason for the changes in funding work in urban areas, according to the then Secretary of State for the Environment, Michael Howard, is that in future local authorities will benefit from 'more than £500 million in additional spending power from capital receipts' (Howard, 1993). However, the Labour MP, Keith Vaz, is highly critical of the government's action, claiming it will lead to thousands of job losses in community work and the closure of community work projects (Vaz, 1993).

As part of its drive to promote closer partnership between industry and public services and to reduce, where possible, the demand on public finance, Conservative administrations from 1979 onwards have encouraged the private sector to support community initiatives (Davies, 1984). However, this remains a minute source of funding, with the 'top 200' companies donating approximately 0.2% of their profits to the community (Davies, 1985), and at the present time 'company giving has ceased to grow' (Association of Researchers and Voluntary Action and Community Involvement, 1992: 12). The economic force of the voluntary sector is, however, powerful. Although it is difficult to collate figures on the number and scope of the voluntary organizations in the United Kingdom, if we take one sector, charities, we find over 168,000 registered in England and Wales. Between them it is estimated that these charities probably employ the equivalent of 250,000 full-time paid staff. The income for these charities exceeds £15 million a year, or over 4% of the gross national product. The charity sector, or 'industry', is three times the size of the agriculture sector, and about the same size as the British car industry (National Council for Voluntary Organisations, 1991: ix).

Finally, although there have been changes in the funding of community work there remains within one important body a strong commitment to funding community development. The Association of Metropolitan Authorities (1993) recognizes that local authorities have a crucial role to play in funding local groups and in employing community workers, usually through intermediary organizations. The Association argues that dissent and debate encourage a healthy, pluralistic democracy, and community work is one activity engaged in this challenging, often ambiguous task.

Community work skills

We discussed in Chapter 3 how the practice theories of community work, of which skills are a central feature, have traditionally been based on pluralist analysis. We also observed that good practice has been defined in terms of technical competence rather than an adherence to particular values and principles. In this way skills are seen as apolitical and 'neutral'. This posits the view that although workers may have competing understandings of the manner in which society is ordered there is agreement on the skills that are used.

It needs to be recognized that while there are a number of case studies (see, for example, Cosgrove and Stevenson, 1985; Cumella, 1983; Morrison, 1984; SCCVO, 1984; Taylor, 1983) and guides to action (see for example Community Action, n.d.; Kinder, 1985; Leissner, 1984; Richardson, 1984; Twelvetrees and Shuttleworth, 1985), there are few texts aimed at assisting community workers with skill development. As mentioned already, a detailed and comprehensive text on community work skills is that by Henderson and Thomas (1987) which, with its focus on neighbourhood work and easily accessible style, is intended for a wider audience than community workers. Two training video tapes have been produced to be used in conjunction with the book.

Henderson and Thomas identify ten stages that neighbourhood work moves through and allocate a section in the book to each. These stages are: entering the neighbourhood; getting to know the neighbourhood; what next?; needs, goals and roles; making contacts and bringing people together; forming and building organizations; helping to clarify goals and priorities; keeping the organization going; dealing with friends and enemies; and leavings and endings. The authors point out that 'the process is not a simple sequential or linear one; most of the stages occur simultaneously with one or some of the others' (Henderson and Thomas, 1987: 27). These different stages suggest different skills required by the worker, the central ones being identified as: contact-making, including meeting members of a community in order to identify their interest in collective action and the contribution and role they might make; group work; locality development; 'putting people in touch with one another, and . . . promoting their membership in groups and networks' (Henderson and Thomas, 1987: 15); negotiation, particularly with decision-makers; and a combination of an understanding of political processes and practical political skills.

Another useful and fairly comprehensive skills manual is that produced by the Association of Community Workers (Harris 1994). Compiled by Val Harris from material written by Association of Community Workers members and by organizations working in the field of community work, it covers a range of areas including community work roles, skills and responsibilities; tackling inequalities; empowerment and participation; getting to know a community; working with groups; conflict in groups; meetings; group organization; volunteers; training; selection and recruitment; supervision; surveys; campaigning; funding; organizing conferences and events; handling information; publications; evaluation; management committees; and local government.

We have noted that advocates of the pluralist approach have indicated that skills can be considered to be 'neutral'. In response, Robertson (1991) warns that skills are not 'neutral' tools and expresses the belief that community workers need to be clear about their own and others' values before practising skills. On the same tack, Dominelli (1990) argues that social problems need redefining in order to acknowledge the power relations that permeate society, particularly those between men and women, and between black and white people. This, she argues, can lead to developing and practising specific skills, as well as sharing skills. Dominelli identified the problems addressed by feminists and the skills needed to implement a successful campaign. She therefore interprets existing skills and demonstrates how they can be used by feminists. For instance, she highlights handling the media as a skill area, and discusses how female community workers can deal with media which attempt to incorporate, sensationalize and ridicule those striving to communicate an alternative or radical viewpoint. Similarly, when collecting data from conventional sources for a particular community, feminists need to highlight the 'significance of gender throughout the process of data collection' and utilize the 'findings in improving women's position' (Dominelli, 1990: 60).

We noted the influence of Freire's writings when evaluating the community education model in Chapter 5. The theory and practice created by this adult educator have been interpreted by a number of practitioners, including Sister Doreen Grant working in the Govan district in Glasgow. In a discussion of her work, Grant (1989) points to the importance of the skills of co-operation, co-ordination and dialogue. Also based on community work in Glasgow, Bryant and Bryant (1982) identify the following skills for a 'good community worker': relationship skills; communication skills; organizational skills; mediating skills; negotiating skills; entrepreneurial skills; research skills; political and analytical skills; and tactical skills. Unlike the work by Henderson and Thomas (1987), the work and writings of Grant and the Bryants claim to be rooted in experiences of working-class communities and areas of economic social deprivation. This leads the writers to state that community workers need to recognize that skills by themselves are insufficient to overcome major structural inequality. However, there is in such communities 'creative scope for helping to unleash capacities for self-organization and political expression amongst citizens who have been previously excluded from the public life of their city' (Bryant and Bryant, 1982: 26).

Our examination above has discovered that there is a debate within the community work field that centres on whether skills are 'neutral'. The pluralist approach indicates that skills are transferable and can be used by practitioners from different ideological perspectives. There are others, notably from the radical, socialist and feminist perspectives, who argue that skills are not 'neutral' but have to be placed alongside and used in tandem with an understanding of the structural nature of society. According to Henderson and Thomas (1987: 22), skills are a tool that can be used in neighbourhood work to 'involve people at grass-roots level in decisions and policies which affect them and their neighbourhoods'.

However, as we have noted throughout our discussions, the focus at the level of the locality has been considered by a number of writers to offer a narrow and an incomplete focus. We have also discovered that a more substantial understanding is available to us if it is recognized that both communities and community work can reflect the class, gender, and racially structured nature of society which distributes power and resources in an inequitable manner. We can further propose, therefore, that for those who believe community work is concerned with challenging societal inequalities, the skills it employs have to be adapted and re-created to address these.

Management

The discussion above on skills leads us finally to explore the management of community work. As we have already noted, a central concern for much of community work practice is the achievement of a more meaningful management of the resources available in a particular community. This could include the management of staff. However, the extent to which this can and does happen is far from clear and, as we will discover with regard to the two fieldwork case studies, such a commitment can be contentious.

One of the problems we have when examining the management of community work is the paucity of material on which to make observations and assessments. This is due in the main to the reticence felt by community workers towards the concepts of management which have often been associated with hierarchical and elitist structures and run counter to activities concerned with participation and the devolution of power. This situation is now changing, with community workers having to accept a 'trade-off' between increased management and further funding. Also there has been a recognition that the management of community work does not necessarily have to be detrimental to the activity, and there are possibilities of developing acceptable forms of management without importing inappropriate methods from the commercial sector.

What does the managing of community resources involve? Taylor (1979: 2) offers a helpful list of tasks which includes 'financial control, policy, fundraising, political protection, hiring and firing, administration, accountability, advice and support to staff, monitoring and evaluation'. This wide remit for management is linked to the diversity of community work managers and the different forms of management. These range from the majority of local authorities which have developed forms of corporate management, and a minority that have pursued decentralization, to community work projects that have *ad hoc* committees or support groups rooted in specific neighbourhoods or localities.

In order for us to progress with this examination of the management of community work I have divided the discussion into two sections. The first section explores the management of projects and workers funded by local authorities, and the second examines the management of voluntary and charitable community work organizations and their workers.

Community work funded by local authorities

The following examination of community work that is sponsored directly by local authorities does not include community work that is funded indirectly by the state via the Urban Programme or any central government department or agency.

The evidence we have from Francis *et al.* (1984), which is the most comprehensive of its type to date, indicates that of those community workers employed by the statutory sector nearly half (47%) are employed by local authority education departments, while 27% are employed in social services departments. Thus between them local authority education and social services departments employ 74% of community workers in the statutory sector. The more recent Bradford survey does not give a percentage breakdown of statutory agencies, although it does note that the youth and community service, the social services, the recreation department and five other significant local authority departments employ 27% of all the respondents (Glenn, 1993).

According to Thomas (1983: 230), workers employed by local authority departments are likely to be engaged in social planning, community organization, and influencing local social policy. Thomas also argues that it is by working within social services departments that community work can influence policies that are 'community oriented'. Also:

> Neighbourhood work may become more valued the more social services develop innovatory attitudes to practice.... Likewise, where social services become more interested in advice- and information-giving roles, working from family and neighbourhood centres, then one would expect continued appreciation of community work.
>
> (Thomas, 1983: 230)

However, this has had implications for the management of community work. Since the Conservatives came to power local authorities have revised, or have been required to revise, their structures as they grapple with new demands on their services and finances. Similarly, local authorities have struggled with calls for them to enhance democracy while being required to operate with technical and financial efficiency (Hampton, 1991: 7). Although these demands are not necessarily incompatible, local authorities have had to accept the Conservative government's introduction of market forces, obliging them, for instance, to tender for services. Although there have been examples of the decentralization of delivery, management and administration of local authority services by Labour-controlled authorities (see the discussions by Hodge, 1987; Hoggett and Hambleton, 1987), and certain Liberal-Democratic Councils, for example, in Tower Hamlets and calls from the political Right for an end to wasteful, inefficient and profligate local govern-ment (Ridley, 1988: 6), the majority of local authorities have met central government demands by continuing to co-ordinate their affairs in a traditional hierarchical and bureaucratic manner. The outcome is that the management of community work within local authorities has followed the dominant trend with the existence of relationships between individuals based upon superiority and subordination, and the imposition of a uniformity of treatment on demands for resources or additional services.

The management of community work ultimately involves accountability and control over it. If that management takes place within a hierarchical structure as local authority community work does, and that activity is a marginal one, then there are implications for the practice. There is evid-ence that community workers employed and managed within local authority departments are usually a constituent part of a team (Barr, 1991). This is in contrast to the situation in the 1970s where workers were often working in isolation (Thomas, 1983: 229). However, in Barr's research the overwhelming response from the community workers interviewed was that their managers wished to impose unnecessary limitations on their work. Further, they felt that their status was considered second-class relative to their social work colleagues. In response, Barr questions whether community work should be located in a department such as social services. He concludes by stating that if local authorities are serious in their commitment to community work they should manage the activity in a manner which

> is consistent with empowering and enabling community organisations to participate and have influence ... Anything less than this promotes contradictions in behaviour of different categories of worker and legit-imates allegations that community work is a token gesture, a sop to the notion of consumer sovereignty.

> (Barr, 1991: 82)

Voluntary and charitable community work

Here I include community work that is funded indirectly by the state via the Urban Programme and government departments, although we are faced with the problem of being unable to examine in detail the different forms of management in the voluntary sector because of the lack of written material.

Historically, the ability to manage community work in more varied ways is greater in the voluntary sector than in the local authority sector, because this is not subject to the pressures that we have discussed above. This has led to a range of different styles of management including self-management or collective working and management (Stanton, 1989), and structureless or leaderless groups and management (Freeman, 1984). However, as we have previously noted, the financing and control of community work has changed in recent years. This has influenced the management of the activity within the voluntary and charitable sector. The figures by Francis et al. (1984) reveal that while the majority of community work takes place in the voluntary sector, the main funding for 85% of all voluntary sector workers comes from the statutory sector. The more recent localized research by Glenn (1993) indicates that although the voluntary sector is the largest employer of community practitioners in Bradford, the major funding sources were the local authority and central government. The greater scrutiny by the state of its funding and the desire to influence and direct the development of community work, have led the government to encourage the major voluntary organizations it funds to concentrate a proportion of their resources in assisting in the development of management training. For instance, the National Council for Voluntary Organizations has taken a prominent position in attempting to improve the management of community work through a range of publications (see, for example, Bolton, 1990; Holloway and Otto, 1988; Leat, 1988; Nathan, 1990; Rogers, 1990), and with the establishment of its Management Development Unit. Similarly the National Youth Agency has tackled the issue through the publication of a series of booklets about managing community-based agencies (see, for example, Feek, 1983a; 1983b; Feek and Smith, 1983), while the Community Development Foundation has produced a number of books and pamphlets on allied topics (Clarke, 1989; Pearse and Smith, 1990).

These organizations and a number of their management publications make a point of emphasizing that attracting state funding is becoming more difficult and that voluntary organizations which have clear objectives and well-defined management structures are the more likely to be in receipt of this declining finance.

Another important issue in the management of community work in the voluntary sector is the role of the principal manager of small voluntary agencies. Peatfield (1992) has made a study of eight voluntary agencies, all of them employing a 'director', 'co-ordinator' or 'organizer' who is responsible to a voluntary committee for the management of the work of a small staff team. Peatfield found that all the managers surveyed suffered a great deal of stress, often related to their complex and ambiguous role and to the small amount of supervision and support they received in their work. The research discovered that in the absence of leadership from their committees the managers assumed the burden of providing their agencies with a sense of direction, often acting as interpreters of unclear policies and procedures. They also frequently had to cope with a wide range of different and often irreconcilable tasks. Peatfield found that managers brought to the position individual 'packages' of interests and experience and considerable commitment to the agency. All those he interviewed had succeeded in developing their own system for ensuring that the work was undertaken successfully. The author suggests that these managers can be seen as successful 'voluntary sector entrepreneurs' whose approach resembles that of a small business owner. However, this success has been achieved at a cost. Peatfield found that managers feel indispensable and are unable to sustain the effort for long periods. This can lead to agencies losing a sense of collective purpose and experiencing difficulties when their manager decides to resign. As a long-term solution, Peatfield suggests that the performance of management committees could be improved. In the meantime, the author argues, agencies should reduce the range of tasks they expect their managers to tackle, and provide them with more systematic induction, supervision and support.

Conclusion

In this chapter we have discussed the central themes in community work practice. Part of the difficulty we experience when examining much of the above work is the lack of satisfactory research into practice. Although there are a number of specific surveys and reports on community work practice, many of these are now dated and often not comprehensive. This gap in the literature has not assisted the development of a coherent theory and practice of community work. We can speculate on the reasons for this gap. One could be the diverse and often ambiguous meanings given to community work. A clearer idea of what comprises community work could assist in the recognition of its areas of practice. Similarly, more research of practice that produces data and evidence could enhance the activity's development. At the present time there are a number of organizations and individuals that do contribute to researching practice and their work has been drawn upon in this chapter. There is, however, a clear need to raise the research profile in community work if we are to appreciate the changes the activity is facing and the development it can make. The results of such work will enable community work to argue more effectively for the scarce resources available in the public sector.

Chapter 7

CONCLUSION AND FUTURE DIRECTIONS

Introduction

The purpose of this book has been to review and evaluate the theories and practice that constitute contemporary community work practice. Throughout the previous discussions we have dealt with theory and practice separately. This has given us the advantage of a rigorous and systematic examination. Although this approach has greatly assisted our exploration, I am aware that the division is in one sense artificial as theory and practice are inextricably linked. This chapter aims to work towards a synthesis while considering the future direction of the activity.

The development and significance of community work theory and practice

The evidence presented in Chapters 2 and 3 confirms that community work lacks a single clear theoretical base. The diversity of tasks and settings, the ebb and flow of the activity's development, and the significant difference in its separate roots, all contribute to our being unable to secure an agreement around one theory and one form of practice. What has emerged are two competing theoretical approaches which have informed practice: the pluralist; and the radical and socialist. These approaches reflect the evolution of community work from benevolent paternalism, on the one hand, and from collective community action, on the other.

In order to examine the development and significance of community work theory and practice it has been important to place the debate within an economic, social and political context. The evidence presented in Chapter 2 indicates that early community work developed in a sporadic fashion. One of the main strands of its early development, benevolent paternalism, emanated mainly from the universities and the Anglican Church. With reference to the development of the settlement movement we recorded how, at the turn of the century, socially concerned philanthropists exercised leadership and influence over selected working-class communities. It has been argued that the settlement movement attempted to improve the quality of life in disadvantaged areas in response to fears of growing dissent between social classes within urban areas. Furthermore, we have noted that settlements were pioneers in a particular form of neighbourhood intervention that was a feature of a wider movement to assist in the conditions for both the creation and the maintenance of British industrial capitalism.

We discussed how, in parallel to benevolent paternalism, collective community action grew both as a form of social protest, and as a vehicle for the development of the organizational and cultural resources of working-class communities. Women and black people also employed the strategy of collective action in their struggles: Women in their campaign for the right to vote and be represented in Parliament, and black people in their demand for independence and freedom from colonial domination.

In the 1960s and 1970s the state involved itself more firmly in initiating and funding community work. It was suggested that this was part of a recognition of the fact that the welfare state had failed to meet the needs of certain communities and individuals, and of capital's continuing requirement for a well-integrated workforce. The two competing ideological strands within community work emerged in different guises. Benevolent paternalism became a reworked form of social democracy, and collective community action developed as a radical and socialist response.

Before moving to consider the significance of pluralist, and radical and socialist theories of community work in contemporary times, we need briefly to refer to our consideration of the impact of the New Right upon the welfare state. We noted that the unpopularity of the welfare state in the 1970s, which was due in part to people's experience of it being bureaucratic, centralised and unfriendly, was a key component in the ascendancy of Thatcherism and the market mechanism as the model for welfare distribution. This became a popular alternative to the theories and practice of social democracy. The generic and contested nature of community work meant it was vulnerable to ideological change, and since 1979 successive administrations have advanced their own interpretation of the practice and its role within the welfare state. However, despite the massive onslaught upon welfare and educational services and the wide-ranging changes seen in both areas, social democracy remains the dominant trend in welfare ideology.

When we consider the role of pluralist theories and practice in contemporary community work we need to refer to the important position held by the 'expert' within social democracy. The 'expert' in the field of social welfare is the social scientist. She/he researches the problems, develops solutions,

organizes the consensus and in many cases manages the organizations that
address the problem. We have observed that since the Second World War
the bulk of community work has been used in just this manner, and this
suggests one reason I posit for the survival of the activity – that is, the state
considers community work as a valuable activity worth supporting in its
need to maintain a presence in vulnerable communities, and in being seen
to address the amelioration of social problems at neighbourhood level.

Moving the argument further, we can consider the role of pressure and
interest groups which pluralists argue to be vital to social democracy. Over
the years the larger community work agencies have been a base for a number
of these groups. For example, settlements, which still exist in many major
cities, have located in them a number of independent projects. The Virginia
House Settlement in Plymouth accommodates various projects and organizations including the Citizens' Advice Bureau and the local Shelter office.
Since its inception in the 1960s, Shelter has attempted to influence governments by seeking to alter the general climate of public opinion around
the issue of housing and homelessness. Similarly, Barton Hill Settlement in
Bristol has been the base for the local branch of the mental health pressure
group, MIND. The existence of a multiplicity of pressure groups is believed
by advocators of pluralism to be an important indicator of the strength of
a pluralist society. The location of pressure groups within community work
projects, therefore, fits comfortably with their pluralist tradition and outlook
and further enhances their profile within a social-democratic state.

Reflecting on the radical and socialist theories that have informed contemporary community work, we have seen that these theories employ an analysis
that highlights poverty and inequality as intrinsic and inevitable aspects of
capitalist social relations. During the 1960s and 1970s radical and socialist
community workers used a class analysis to advocate the possibility of far-
reaching changes in society. Community action was considered to be one
vehicle in this radical movement. The work of Gough (1979) and the London Edinburgh Weekend Return Group (1980) further developed socialist
theories and indicated the contradictory nature of the welfare state and the
recognition that state employees, including community workers, could find
oppositional space to change the social relations within the welfare state.
The developing theories of feminism, and in particular socialist feminism,
and the black and anti-racist critique, have challenged masculist and white
perspectives on community work. We analysed the impact of these theories
and critiques and found them to provide significant explanations of British
society.

It was concluded in our earlier discussion that the debates on the development of different community work theories are intrinsically insular and
specific. In response, and as part of the task of invigorating the theoretical
underpinning of community work, consideration was given to a number
of key perspectives which could assist in a more informed theory of the
activity.

We began by analysing the work of Antonio Gramsci. It is his insights into and interpretations of hegemony, ideology and intellectuals that are considered relevant to contemporary practice. Using Gramsci's theoretical work, we were able to suggest that community workers occupy a contradictory position within the state apparatus. This position provides them with opportunities to create conditions to assist members of communities to articulate their own contradictory experiences and understandings of the world. With this interpretation of the role community work can play in contemporary society we considered urban and new social movements. It was discovered that a study of the implications of the role of social movements, together with the lessons learnt from Gramsci, offered the possibility of a more critical community work theory and practice. I have suggested that theoretically and practically it may be possible to challenge background assumptions that permeate social relations. At the same time, the community worker needs to be aware of the wider developments within society, including those at a global level, which connect with the local community's daily experiences. Finally, it was noted that unless these factors are recognized community work will only ever be a neighbourhood activity.

Community work models

My review of community work models revealed a number that assist in classifying in a more orderly manner the wide range of activity termed 'community work'. It was found that the most readily agreed upon models were: community care; community organization; community development; social/community planning; community education; and community action. We also considered models that have been developed from feminist community work theory and the black and anti-racist critique. Although the models are a helpful way of categorizing community work, it was recognized that they are fundamentally a method of exploring the diversity of the work. There is therefore a degree of overlap between them. We found that a useful method of categorizing the models is to place them on a continuum that moves from models primarily focused upon 'care' to those that emphasize 'action'.

Our discussion of models in Chapter 5 led to consideration of an important question. Can a community worker with a particular ideology successfully and satisfactorily work within an organization that is modelled in a way that is at odds with her/his own view of the world? Evidence from the literature indicates that community work posts offer practitioners the opportunity of practising in a manner close to their own values. Community work, for example, provides practitioners with less prescriptive ways of working with individuals and groups than those offered by social work. However, my experience indicates that there are differing degrees of satisfaction as to whether agencies allow workers fully to exercise their values and beliefs. This is particularly so during a period of public expenditure cutbacks and the imposition of regulatory apparatus aimed at increasing the influence of market principles. Nevertheless, as the surveys on practitioners have indicated, community workers often sacrifice the opportunity to earn larger salaries in other forms of work for the greater independence offered by their present employment. As we know, though, this employment has the drawback of being insecurely financed. The freedom to practise in a particular manner, therefore, is determined by a number of factors including the financing of the agency and its overall philosophy. In view of this, the key would seem to be the climate within the agency. If critical discussion is encouraged and workers' opinions are welcomed then open debate can lead to a satisfactory working environment where progressive and innovative work can prosper. If the reverse is the case and practitioners perceive their views as unwelcome or ignored, and themselves as marginalized, then they may leave to seek opportunities that can accommodate their view and style of working.

The conclusion that can be drawn here is that models employed by agencies depend upon a complex range of variables including local traditions, agency management and philosophy, funding, and the theories held by the employees. Where there is a divergence between the agency's interpretation of the work and the model employed, on the one hand, and the theories that inform practitioners, on the other, there are possibilities for conflict and dissatisfaction.

Community care and community development

Returning to our discussion of the community care model, we have noted that the rapid development of this form of working is due to the priority given it by the government as part of its community care policy. Community work has a role to play in this area, but not in the manner envisaged by the 1990 National Health Service and Community Care Act. Community care as seen by the Act is about the assessment of individual needs and managing provision to meet those needs. Overall, it is about the work of staff in the caring services rather than about care *by* the community. An innovative approach would be to employ community development strategies. The 1990 Act requires joint planning to take place between local and health authorities and the voluntary sector, examining a range of services and approaches outside those traditionally provided. A community development approach to the implementation of the Act could lead to the empowerment of users and the involvement of small community groups. As we have already observed, there are problems associated with this including the exploitation of carers (the majority of whom are women), the lack of democracy in the organization and delivery of community care, and the provision of poor services for poor people. There is potential, however, in examining this area of work, particularly if community development strategies could be deployed to support self-help organizations and assist in skills development. Mayo (1994) provides an excellent discussion on the dilemmas encountered by community care. She raises a number of pertinent questions; in particular, she asks, if adequate provision is not an option, what is the real value of community participation and choice? The difficulties and contradictions inherent in the delivery of community care and the role of community development should not be underestimated. The crux of any involvement of community development in this way must be to understand fully the limitations of such work and the need to link debates at the local level with an agenda for social and economic change.

Freire and Gramsci: a critical way forward

We recognized in Chapter 5 the theories and practice of Paulo Freire as helpful to radical community education. We also noted the influential writings of Antonio Gramsci and their potential for an understanding of the role and function of community work in a capitalist society. I now examine how the ideas of these two writers can be taken forward in the theory and practice of community work. To do this I have placed the debate within a personal account of how I came to encounter these two writers and the contribution they have made to my own learning and understanding.

While I was employed as a community work practitioner in Birmingham in the 1970s the British social, political and economic fabric was undergoing a radical change. The Labour government began to cut away at the social wage in its attempt to shore up the value of sterling and to pay off massive loans to the International Monetary Fund. My work with some of the poorest citizens of Birmingham, and in particular sections of the black population, meant that I saw for myself how the effects of large-scale public expenditure cuts and the insidious nature of racism, sexism and classism were affecting people in already disadvantaged communities. The analysis I had developed based on Fabian thinking and social-democratic ideals became untenable when the very people for whom we were supposed to be working were having their life chances reduced by circumstances completely outside their control. In turn, I rejected the orthodox Marxist position as it failed to connect with my own growing understanding of the problems faced by vulnerable communities. I found the orthodox Marxist view essentially negative, claiming that the welfare state was a monolithic structure that exercised social control over the working class. In this view community work was one of a range of mechanisms aimed at exploiting and maintaining people within a certain hierarchical structure. Orthodox Marxism claimed that people were powerless to change the status quo unless they gathered together in a revolutionary party aimed at altering the economic system. In an attempt to understand the situation that was unfolding, almost in front of my own eyes, I looked around for an intellectual analysis that resonated with my own struggle to retain a degree of optimism and hope in the most difficult of circumstances. It was at this stage I commenced reading Freire's work and began to appreciate his ideas of the 'banking' system of education and the potential people have in transcending their own situations. Further reading and then study during the late 1970s in the Department of Applied Social Studies at the University of Warwick led me to the work of Gramsci. By then my understanding of the black struggle was more developed and my appreciation of the value of feminist thinking clearer.

As Thatcherism began to take hold in Britain and was exported to other social democracies and former totalitarian systems it became apparent that there was unlikely to be any major change in the way Britain was going to be governed for many years to come. It was then that I noted the impact of social movements, and in particular new social movements, upon the social systems in western and eastern European countries. As Western industrialized societies began radically changing, and as the international economies began a shift of emphasis from manufacturing and production to service economies and 'knowledge industries', a space began opening up in the social world which challenged the traditional power (including political) structures. In eastern Europe the various revolts against communist rule reflected a comparatively well-developed alternative political structure built upon a network of workers, intellectuals and students. In Britain we witnessed campaigns against Clause 28 of the Local Government Act 1988 which prevents local authorities from 'promoting' homosexuality, as well as local and national struggles against assaults aimed at radically changing or dismantling the National Health Service, the social security system, pensions, school meals, public transport and child benefit. Perhaps the two most prominent national campaigns were the Greenham Common women's peace camp, which moved million's world-wide in their protest against the proliferation of nuclear warheads, and the campaign against the poll tax which led eventually to Margaret Thatcher's fall from office. What became increasingly clear to me was the analysis that the writings of Freire and Gramsci could bring to these events. Freire's emphasis on cultural action demonstrated that people, organized collectively and with a common understanding, could effect outcomes within a society. Gramsci's work, meanwhile, reflected the view that radical change does not come about only in the economic sphere, but can also result from struggle in civil society. It is perhaps Gramsci's most famous statement of the 'pessimism of the intellect and the optimism of the will' that inspired me to consider the opportunities within community work rather than to cave in and accept the reactionary Thatcherite period. What both writers offered me was an alternative to the determinist and monolithic view of the state, one that focuses upon struggle and contradiction. Both stress the importance of hope in defeating the fatalisms of the present. However, as we know, such hope has to be rooted in a critical reflection on the lessons of past struggles.

If community workers truly want to assist people to liberate and empower themselves, they can gain much from reading and reflecting upon the work of Freire and Gramsci. They are both inspirational in their message that change is possible if one is clear about one's goals and strategies. Gramsci offers a tenable macro-view of capitalist relations. Freire provides a guide to practice that can assist in liberating those negatively affected by capitalism. Both offer us a critical way forward.

Further research

I have noted at different places in this book the paucity of literature and research in the community work field. This was one of my own driving forces in writing the book. I now offer two areas that would benefit from further exploration.

Firstly, my examination has documented the general inappropriateness of aspects of community work theory. While being aware of examples of useful elements of different theories, I am conscious that a good deal of the literature relating to this area is a decade old or more and does not address contemporary themes. In relation to this, therefore, I suggest further development of community work theory on similar lines to those introduced above. I have concluded that Gramsci's theories have a part to play in assisting radical community work to revitalize its theoretical position. Further research could use this as a theoretical framework that could then consider aspects of practice, where Gramsci's work appears less helpful. Similarly, we have explored the work of Freire and noted how it provides a valuable guide to pluralist and radical practice. Research could usefully be undertaken that assists in the evolution of a community work theory and practice based on these two significant writers.

My other suggestion for a future research focus is with regard to models. Our investigation has alerted us to the growth in the use of the community care model in community work. The concern for a number of community workers must be whether this will lead to a diminution of models where 'action' rather than 'care' is a central feature. Research that analyses and categorizes in more detail the changing nature of community work models will further our understanding of the activity's development.

Community work training

We have discussed the lack of any national award for those who complete appropriate community work training courses. This fact, of course, has not gone unrecognized in community work circles, which have spent considerable time and energy discussing the advantages and disadvantages of such an award. Discussions have moved at speed and it is possible that I have been unable fully to reflect the changing picture in this respect. However, if community work is to move from its marginal position within the welfare and educational services, and attempt to secure more satisfactory funding than it has hitherto been able to achieve, it needs to demonstrate that it is able to train its workers effectively. One of the main conclusions I have drawn from talking with scores of community workers over the last few years is that they wish to be updated with skills and knowledge appropriate for these changing times. In making this recommendation, I am aware of the contradiction this leads to where further state finance leads to greater state control. An overriding concern must be that without clear, well-resourced training courses, community work is vulnerable to take-over by forces that do not share its unique, if contested, meaning and purpose.

And finally

I started this book with the intention of helping to sharpen community work's critical edge, to increase its critical analysis and to assist in its practice. This all sounds very grand. Nevertheless, I hope that in a small measure I have pushed the boat out for a more developed and critical examination of the activity. Community work remains a powerful and unique form of practice for those who wish to engage in work with communities. The key for practitioners and educators alike is to appreciate and embrace this, and to continue to strive for the development of an effective and relevant community work theory and practice.

REFERENCES

Abel-Smith, B. and Townsend, P. (1965). *The Poor and the Poorest*. London: Bell.

Abrams, P. (1978). *Work, Urbanism and Inequality: UK Society Today*. London: Weidenfeld & Nicolson.

Adamson, N., Briskin, L. and McPhail, M. (1988). *Organizing for Change: The Contemporary Women's Movement in Canada*. Oxford: Oxford University Press.

Adeyemi, F. (1985). 'The Abolition of the G.L.C.: The Implications for the Black Community', *Talking Point*, no. 65. Newcastle upon Tyne: Association of Community Workers.

Alinsky, S. (1969). *Reveille for Radicals*. New York: Vintage Books.

Alinsky, S. (1971). *Rules for Radicals*. New York: Random House.

Allen, G., Bastiani, J., Martin, I. and Richards, K. (eds) (1987). *Community Education: An Agenda for Educational Reform*. Milton Keynes: Open University Press.

Allen, G. and Martin, I. (eds) (1992) *Education and Community: The Politics of Practice*. London: Cassell.

Allen, S. and Wolkowitz, C. (1986). 'The Control of Women's Labour: The Case of Homeworking', *Feminist Review* 22, Spring: 25–51.

Allman, P. (1987). 'Paulo Freire's Education: A Struggle for Meaning' in Allen, G., Bastiani, J., Martin, I. and Richards, K. (eds), *Community Education: An Agenda for Educational Reform*. Milton Keynes: Open University Press.

Amin, K. and Leech, K. (1988). 'A New Underclass: Race and Poverty in the Inner City' in *Poverty 70*. London: Child Poverty Action Group.

Anionwu, E. (1990). 'Community Development Approaches to Sickle Cell Anaemia', *Talking Point*, no. 113. Newcastle upon Tyne: Association of Community Workers.

Anthony, P. (1983). *John Ruskin's Labour*. Cambridge: Cambridge University Press.

Anwar, M. (1986). *Race and Politics, Ethnic Minorities and the British Political System*. London: Tavistock.

Armstrong, L. (1987). *Kiss Daddy Goodnight*. New York: Random House.

Asian Sheltered Residential Accommodation (1981). *Asian Sheltered Residential Accommodation.* London: Asian Sheltered Residential Accommodation.

Association of Community Workers (1982). *ACW Definition of Community Work.* London: Association of Community Workers.

Association of Community Workers (1991). 'New National Community Work Training Proposals', *Talking Point*, no. 125. Newcastle upon Tyne: Association of Community Workers.

Association of Metropolitan Authorities (1993). *Local Authorities and Community Development: A Strategic Opportunity for the 1990s.* London: AMA.

Association of Researchers in Voluntary Action and Community Involvement (1991). 'Damaging Those It Is Meant To Help', *AVRAC Bulletin*, no. 45, Summer. Wivenhoe: Association of Researchers in Voluntary Action and Community Involvement.

Association of Researchers in Voluntary Action and Community Involvement (1992). 'Local Authority Funding for Voluntary Organisations', *AVRAC Bulletin* no. 50, Autumn. Wivenhoe: Association of Researchers in Voluntary Action and Community Involvement.

Bagguley, P. (1991). *From Protest to Acquiescence? Political Movements of the Unemployed.* Basingstoke: Macmillan.

Baine, S., Bennington, J. and Russell, J. (1992). *Changing Europe: Challenges Facing the Voluntary and Community Sectors in the 1990's.* London: National Council for Voluntary Organisations Publications and the Community Development Foundation.

Baldock, P. (1977). 'Why Community Action? The Historical Origins of the Radical Trend in British Community Work', *Community Development Journal*, 12(3): 172–81.

Barclay, P.M. (1982). *Social Workers: Their Role and Tasks (The Barclay Report).* London: Bedford Square Press.

Barker, A. (1981). 'Strategy and Style in Local Community Relations' in Cheetham, J., James, W., Loney, M., Mayor, B. and Prescott, W. (eds), *Social and Community Work in a Multi-racial Society.* London: Harper & Row.

Barker, H. (1986). 'Recapturing Sisterhood: A Critical Look at 'Process' in Feminist Organising and Community Work', *Critical Social Policy*, 16, Summer: 80–90.

Barnett, S.A. (1888). *Practicable Socialism.* London: Longmans, Green & Co.

Barnett, S.A. (1904). *Towards Social Reform.* London: T. Fisher & Unwin.

Barr, A. (1991). *Practising Community Development: Experience in Strathclyde.* London: Community Development Foundation.

Batten, T.R. (1957). *Communities and Their Development.* London: Oxford University Press.

Batten, T.R. (1962). *Training for Community Development: A Critical Study of Method.* London: Oxford University Press.

Batten, T.R. (1965). *The Human Factor in Community Work.* London: Oxford University Press.

Batten, T.R., with the collaboration of Madge Batten (1967). *The Non-directive Approach in Group and Community Work.* London: Oxford University Press.

Bédarida, F. (1990). *A Social History of England 1851–1990* (translated by Forster, A.S. and Hodgkinson, J.). London: Routledge.

Beilharz, P. (1992). *Labour's Utopias: Bolshevism, Fabianism, Social Democracy.* London: Routledge.

Bell, C. and Newby, H. (1971). *Community Studies.* London: Allen & Unwin.

Benfield, G. (1990). *Rural Deprivation and Community Work.* Swansea: School of Social Studies, University of Swansea and the Community Development Foundation.

Ben-Tovim, G., Gabriel, J., Law, I. and Stedder, K. (1986). *The Local Politics of Race.* London: Macmillan.

Benyon, J. and Solomos, J. (1987). *The Roots of Urban Unrest.* Oxford: Pergamon Press.

Berer, M. (1988). 'Whatever Happened to A Woman's Right to Choose?', *Feminist Review*, 29, Spring: 24–37.

Beresford, P. and Croft, S. (1986). *Whose Welfare? Private Care or Public Services*. Brighton: The Lewis Cohen Urban Studies Centre at Brighton Polytechnic.

Bhat, A., Carr-Hill, R. and Ohri, S. (eds) (1988). *Britain's Black Population: A New Perspective* (2nd edn). Aldershot: Gower.

Bhavnani, K. (1982). 'Racist Acts', *Spare Rib*, 117, April.

Bhavnani, R. (1986). 'The Struggle for an Anti-racist Policy in Education in Avon', *Critical Social Policy*, 16: 104–8.

Biddle, L. and Biddle, W. (1965). *The Community Development Process: The Rediscovery of Local Initiative*. New York: Holt, Rinehart & Winston.

Binney, V., Harkell, G. and Nixon, J. (1981). *Leaving Violent Men: A Study of Refugees and Housing for Battered Women*. London: Women's Aid Federation.

Birke, J. (1986). *Women, Feminism and Biology: The Feminist Challenge*. Brighton: Wheatsheaf.

Black, A. (1988). *State, Community and Human Desire*. Brighton: Harvester Wheatsheaf.

Bloomfield, B. (1986). 'Women's Support Groups at Maerdy' in Samuel, R., Bloomfield, B. and Boanas, G. (eds), *The Enemy Within: Pit Villages and the Miners Strike of 1984–5*. London: Routledge & Kegan Paul.

Boddy, M. (1984). 'Local Economic and Employment Strategies' in Boddy, M. and Fudge, C. (eds), *Local Socialism?* London: Macmillan.

Bogdanor, Y. and Skidelsky, R. (1970). *The Age of Affluence, 1951–64*. London: Macmillan.

Bolger, S. and Scott, D. (1984). *Starting from Strengths: The Report of the Panel to Promote the Continuing Development of Training for Part Time and Voluntary Youth and Community Work*. Leicester: National Youth Bureau.

Bolger, S., Corrigan, P., Docking, J. and Frost, N. (1981). *Towards Socialist Welfare Work*. London: Macmillan.

Bolt, C. and Drescher, S. (eds) (1980). *Anti-slavery, Religion and Reform*. Folkestone: William Dawson & Sons.

Bolton, C. (1990). *The Role and Management Development of Chief Executives in Small Voluntary Organisations*. London: National Council for Voluntary Organisations.

Braham, P., Rattansi, A. and Skellington, R. (eds) (1992). *Racism and Anti-racism: Inequality, Opportunities and Policies*. London: Sage/Open University.

Brandwein, R.A. (1987). 'Women and Community Organisation' in Burden, D.S. and Gottlieb, N. (eds), *The Woman Client*. London: Tavistock.

Briggs, A. and Macartney, A. (1984). *Toynbee Hall: The First Hundred Years*. London: Routledge & Kegan Paul.

Brown, A. (1986). *Groupwork*. London: Heinemann Educational Books.

Bryan, B., Dadzie, S. and Scafe, S. (1985). *The Heart of the Race: Black Women's Lives in Britain*. London: Virago.

Bryant, B. and Bryant, R. (1982). *Change and Conflict: A Study of Community Work in Glasgow*. Aberdeen: Aberdeen University Press.

Bryers, P. (1979). 'The Development of Practice Theory in Community Work'. *Community Development Journal*, 14(3): 200–09.

Buckingham, G. and Martin, M. (1989). 'Community Development, Harassment and Racism', *Talking Point*, no. 103. Newcastle upon Tyne: Association of Community Workers.

Burns, D. (1992). *Poll Tax Rebellion*. Stirling and London: AK Press and Attack International.

Burrows, L. and Walentowicz, P. (1992). *Homes Cost Less Than Homelessness*. London: Shelter.

Butcher, H. (1986). 'The Community Practice Approach to Local Public Provision: An Analysis of Recent Developments', *Community Development Journal*, 21(2): 107–15.

Butcher, H. (1992). 'Community Work: Current Realities, Contemporary Trends' in Carter, P., Jeffs, T. and Smith, M.K. (eds), *Changing Social Work and Welfare*. Buckingham: Open University Press.

Butcher, H., Law, I.G., Leach, R. and Mullard, M. (1990). *Local Government and Thatcherism*. London: Routledge.

Butcher, H., Glen, A., Henderson, P. and Smith, J. (1993). *Community and Public Policy*. London: Pluto Press in association with the Community Development Foundation and Bradford and Ilkley Community College.

Butler, D. and Sloman, A. (1976). *British Political Facts, 1900–1975*. London: Macmillan.

CDP (1977). *Gilding the Ghetto: The State and The Poverty Experiments*. London: Community Development Project Inter-project Editorial Team.

CPAG (1988). *Poverty: The Facts* (2nd edn). London: Child Poverty Action Group.

Calder, A. (1971). *The People's War*. London: Panther.

Calouste Gulbenkian Foundation (1968). *Community Work and Social Change*. London: Longman.

Cameron, C., Lush, A. and Meara, G. (1943). *Disinherited Youth*. Edinburgh: Carnegie United Kingdom.

Campbell, B. (1993). 'Stand of a Local Heroine', *Guardian*, 25 January.

Carey, S. and Shukur, A. (1985–6). 'A Profile of the Bangladeshi Community in East London' in *New Community*, 12(3): 405–17.

Carr-Hill, R. and Chadha-Boreham, H. (1988). 'Education' in Bhat, A., Carr-Hill, R. and Ohri, S. (eds), *Britain's Black Population: A New Perspective* (2nd edn). Aldershot: Gower.

Carter, T. (1986). *Shattering Illusions*. London: Lawrence & Wishart.

Castells, M. (1975). 'Advanced Capitalism, Collective Consumption and Urban Contradictions' in Lindberg, L., Alford, R., Crouch, C. and Offe, C. (eds), *Stress and Contradictions in Modern Capitalism*. London: Lexington Books.

Castells, M. (1977). *The Urban Question*. London: Edward Arnold.

Castells, M. (1983). *The City and the Grassroots*. London: Edward Arnold.

Central Council for Education and Training in Social Work (1992). *CCETSW News*, No. 4, Spring. London: Central Council for Education and Training in Social Work.

Chanan, G. and Vos, K. (1989). *Social Change and Local Action: Coping with Disadvantage in Urban Areas*. London: European Foundation for the Improvement of Living and Working Conditions.

Cheetham, J. (1988). 'Ethnic Associations in Britain' in Jenkins, S. (ed.), *Ethnic Associations and the Welfare State*. New York: Columbia University Press.

Clark, D. (1983). 'The Concept of Community Education', *Journal of Community Education*, 2(3): 34–41.

Clarke, S. (1989). *Seeing It Through: How to Be Effective on a Committee*. London: Community Development Foundation/Bedford Square Press.

Cliffe, D. (1985). *Community Work in Leicester*. Leicester: University of Leicester Centre for Mass Communication Research.

Coates, K. and Silburn, R. (1970). *Poverty: The Forgotten Englishmen*. Harmondsworth: Penguin.

Cockburn, C. (1977). *The Local State*. London: Pluto Press.

Cockburn, C. (1991). *In the Way of Women: Men's Resistance to Sex Equality in Organizations*. Basingstoke: Macmillan.

Cochrane, A. (1993). *Whatever Happened to Local Government?* Buckingham: Open University Press.

Cole, G.D.H. (1918). *Self Government in Industry*. London: Bell.

Cole, G.D.H. (1920). *Guild Socialism Re-stated*. London: Parsons.

Cole, M.I. (ed.) (1956). *Beatrice Webb's Diaries 1924–1932*. London: Fabian Society.

Coleman, D.A. (1987). 'UK Statistics on Immigration: Development and Limitations', *Immigration Migration Review*, 21, Winter: 1137–52.

Community Action (n.d.). *Investigator's Handbook: A Guide for Tenants, Workers and Action Groups on How to Investigate Companies, Organisations and Individuals*. London: Community Action.

Convention of Scottish Local Authorities (1990). *Recommendations for the Way Forward in the Identification of Standards Linked to Vocational Qualifications: Community Work Feasibility Study*. London: Core Sector Consortium Voluntary Organisations Group (based at the National Council for Voluntary Organisations (Advice Development Team), Regent's Wharf, 8 All Saints Street, London N1 9RL).

Cook, A. and Kirk, G. (1983). *Greenham Women Everywhere: Dreams, Ideas and Action from the Women's Peace Movement*. London: Pluto Press.

Corkey, D. and Craig, G. (1978). 'Community Work or Class Politics?' in Curno, P. (ed.), *Political Issues and Community Work*. London: Routledge & Kegan Paul.

Cornwell, J. (1984). *Hard Earned Lives*. London: Tavistock.

Corrigan, P. and Ginsburg, N. (1975). 'Tenants' Struggle and Class Struggle' in Political Economy of Housing Workshop, *Political Economy and the Housing Question*. London: Octopress.

Cosgrove, J. and Stevenson, M. (1985). 'The Work of the Leith Community Education Project', *Liberal Education*, 53, Summer: 20–22.

Council for Education and Training in Youth and Community Work (1989). *Guidelines to Endorsement: Initial Training in Youth and Community Work*. Leicester: Council for Education and Training in Youth and Community Work.

Council of Europe (1989). *Proceedings of Twenty Fourth Session March 7–9*. Strasbourg: Council of Europe.

Coutts, K. and Godley, W. (1989). 'The British Economy under Mrs Thatcher', *Political Quarterly*, Summer, 60(2): 137–51.

Cowley, J., Kaye, A., Mayo, M. and Thompson, M. (1977). *Community or Class Struggle*. London: Stage 1.

Craig, G. (1989). 'Community Work and the State', *Community Development Journal*, 24(1): 3–18.

Craig, G., Mayo, M. and Sharman, N. (1979). *Jobs and Community Action: Community Work Five*. London: Routledge & Kegan Paul in association with the Association of Community Workers.

Craig, G., Derricourt, N. and Loney, M. (eds) (1982). *Community Work and the State: Towards a Radical Practice: Community Work Eight*. London: Routledge & Kegan Paul in association with the Association of Community Workers.

Croft, S. (1986). 'Women, Caring and the Recasting of Need', *Critical Social Policy*, 16: 23–39.

Cumella, M. (1983). 'The Changing Face of British Community Work: the Polypill Community Project in South Wales', *COMM*, 19, September. Marcinelle, Belgium: Inter-University European Institute of Social Welfare, rue du Debarcadère 179, B-6001 Marcinelle.

Cumella, M. (1984). 'Community Work and Unemployment – The Aftermath of the "Slimline" of the Steel Industry in Newport, South Wales', *COMM*, 22, August. Marcinelle, Belgium: Inter-University European Institute of Social Welfare, rue du Debarcadère, 179, B-6001 Marcinelle.

Curno, A., Lamming, A., Leach, L., Stiles, J., Ward, V. and Ziff, T. (1982). *Women in Collective Action*. Newcastle upon Tyne: Association of Community Workers.

Curno, P. (ed.) (1978). *Political Issues and Community Work: Community Work Four*. London: Routledge & Kegan Paul.

DES (1967). *Children and Their Primary Schools*. Report to the Central Advisory Council for Education, No. 1 (Plowden Report). London: HMSO.

DES (1969) *Youth and Community Work in the 1970s. Proposals by the Youth Service Development Council* (Fairbairn-Milson Report). London: HMSO.

DHSS (1989). *Caring for People – Community Care in the Next Decade and Beyond*. London: HMSO.

Dalley, G. (1988). *Ideologies of Caring: Rethinking Community and Collectivism*. London: Macmillan.

Damer, S. (1980). 'State, Class and Housing: Glasgow 1875–1919' in Melling, J. (ed.), *Housing, Social Policy and the State*. London: Croom Helm.

Davies, R. (1984). 'Company Cash and a Whole Lot More'. *Voluntary Action*, 2, 8 October.

Davies, R. (1985). 'How Voluntary Organisations Can Benefit from Business', *NCVO Information Sheet*, 30, January. London: National Council for Voluntary Organisations.

Dearlove, J. (1974). 'The Control of Change and the Regulations of Community Action' in Jones, D. and Mayo, M. (eds), *Community Work One*. London: Routledge & Kegan Paul.

Demuth, C. (1977). *Government Initiatives on Urban Deprivation*. London: Runnymede Trust.

Directory of Social Change (1992). *Funding Black Groups*. London: Directory of Social Change.

Dixon, G., Johnson, C., Leigh, S. and Turnbull, N. (1982). 'Feminist Perspectives and Practice' in Craig, G., Derricourt, N. and Loney, M. (eds), *Community Work and the State: Towards a Radical Practice: Community Work Eight*. London: Routledge & Kegan Paul.

Dolby, N. (1987). *Norma Dolby's Diary*. London: Verso.

Dominelli, L. (1986). 'Father–Daughter Incest: Patriarchy's Shameful Secret', *Critical Social Policy*, 16: 8–22.

Dominelli, L. (1989). 'Betrayal of Trust: A Feminist Analysis of Power Relationships in Incest Abuse', *British Journal of Social Work*, 19(4): 291–302.

Dominelli, L. (1990). *Women and Community Action*. Birmingham: Venture Press.

Dominelli, L. (1994). 'Women, Community Work and the State in the 1990s' in Jacobs, S. and Popple, K. (eds), *Community Work in the 1990s*. Nottingham: Spokesman.

Dominelli, L. and McLeod, E. (1989). *Feminist Social Work*. London: Macmillan.

Doyal, L. and Elston, M.A. (1986). 'Women, Health and Medicine' in Beechey, V. and Whitelegg, E. (eds), *Women in Britain Today*. Milton Keynes: Open University Press.

Dummett, A. (ed.) (1986). *Towards a Just Immigration Policy*. London: The Cobden Trust.

Dunleavy, P. (1980). *Urban Political Analysis*. London: Macmillan.

Edwards, J. and Batley, R. (1978). *The Politics of Positive Discrimination*. London: Tavistock.

Ellison, D. (1988). 'Community Work and E.T.', *Talking Point*, no. 98, November. Newcastle upon Tyne: Association of Community Workers.

Equal Opportunities Commission (1984). *Carers and Services: A Comparison of Men and Women Caring for Dependent Elderly People*. Manchester: Equal Opportunities Commission.

Equal Opportunities Commision (1986). *Annual Report*. Manchester: Equal Opportunities Commission.

Fairbairn, A. (1979). *The Leicestershire Community Colleges and Centres*. Nottingham: Nottingham University/National Institute for Adult Education.

Family Policy Studies Centre (1989). *Family Policy Bulletin*, no. 6. London: Family Policy Studies Centre.

Fawzi El-Solh, C. (1991). 'Somalis in London's East End: A Community Striving for Recognition', *New Community*, 17(4): 539–52.

Federation of Community Work Training Groups (1991). *Proposals for Community Work Training and Qualifications*. Sheffield: Federation of Community Work Training Groups.

Federation of Community Work Training Groups (1992). *Community Work Forum of Interest Proposal for Community Work Training and Qualifications Update, April 1992*. Sheffield: Federation of Community Work Training Groups.

Feek, W. (1983a). *Who Takes the Strain? The Choices for Staff Support*. Leicester: National Youth Agency.

Feek, W. (1983b). *Steps in Time: A Guide to Agency Planning*. Leicester: National Youth Agency.

Feek, W. and Smith, D.I. (1983). *Value Judgements: Evaluating Community-based Agencies*. Leicester: National Youth Agency.

Feminism and Non-Violence Study Group (1983). *Piecing it Together: Feminism and Non-violence*. Buckleigh: Feminism and Non-Violence Group.

Finch, J. (1982). 'A Women's Health Group in Mansfield' in Curno, A., Lamming, A., Leach, L., Stiles, J., Ward, V. and Ziff, T. (eds), *Women in Collective Action*. Newcastle upon Tyne: Association of Community Workers.

Finch, J. (1984). 'Community Care: Developing Non-sexist Alternatives', *Critical Social Policy*, 9: 6–18.

Finch, J. and Groves, D. (eds) (1983). *A Labour of Love: Women, Work and Caring*. London: Routledge & Kegan Paul.

Finch, J. and Groves, D. (1985). 'Community Care and the Family: A Case for Equal Opportunities' in Ungerson, C. (ed.), *Women and Social Policy: A Reader*. London: Macmillan.

Finch, S., with Mary, Cynthia, Linda, Colleen, Barbara and Jan, from Hackney Greenham Group (1986). 'Socialist Feminism and Greenham', *Feminist Review*, 23, Summer: 93–100.

Finn, D. (1987). *Training without Jobs: New Deals and Broken Promises*. London: Macmillan.

Flynn, P., Johnson, C., Lieberman, S. and Armstrong, H. (1986). *You're Learning All The Time: Women, Education and Community Work*. Nottingham: Spokesman.

Foot, P. (1969). *The Rise of Enoch Powell: An Examination of Enoch Powell's Attitude to Immigration and Race*. Harmondsworth: Penguin.

Forrest, D. (1984). 'Marxism and the Community Worker', *Talking Point*, no. 50. Newcastle upon Tyne: Association of Community Workers.

Foucault, M. (1967). *Madness and Civilisation: A History of Insanity*. London: Tavistock.

Foucault, M. (1977). *Discipline and Punishment: The Birth of the Prison*. Harmondsworth: Allen Lane.

Foucault, M. (1988). 'The Ethic of Care for the Self as a Practice of Freedom' in Bernauer, J. and Rasmussen, D. (eds), *The Final Foucault*. Cambridge, Mass.: MIT Press.

Foucault, M. (1989). 'The Return of Morality' in Lotringer, S. (ed.), *Foucault Live*. New York: Semiotext.

Francis, D. and Henderson, P. (1992). *Working with Rural Communities*. Basingstoke: Macmillan.

Francis, D. and Henderson, P. (1993). *Community Development and Rural Issues*. London: Community Development Foundation.

Francis, D., Henderson, P. and Thomas, D.N. (1984). *A Survey of Community Workers in the United Kingdom*. London: National Institute for Social Work.

Frankenberg, R. (1969). *Communities in Britain: Social Life in Town and Country*. Harmondsworth: Penguin Books.

Fraser, D. (1984). *The Evolution of the British Welfare State* (2nd edn). London: Macmillan.

Fraser, J. (1987). 'Community: The Private and the Individual'. *Journal of Sociological Review*, 35(4): 795–818.

Fraser, N. (1989). *Unruly Practices: Power, Discourse and Gender in Contemporary Social Theory*. Cambridge: Polity.

Freeman, J. (1984). *The Tyranny of Structurelessness*. London: Dark Star and Rebel Press.

Freire, P. (1970). *Cultural Action for Freedom*. Harmondsworth: Penguin.

Freire, P. (1972). *Pedagogy of the Oppressed*. Harmondsworth: Penguin.

Freire, P. (1976). *Education: The Practice of Freedom*. London: Writers and Readers Publishing Cooperative.

Freire, P. (1985). *The Politics of Education: Culture, Power and Liberation*. London: Macmillan.

Fromm, E. (1969) *Escape From Freedom*. New York: Avon Books.

Fryer, P. (1984). *Staying Power: The History of Black People in Britain*. London: Pluto Press.

Gallacher, A. (1977). 'Women and Community Work' in Mayo, M. (ed.), *Women in the Community*. London: Routledge & Kegan Paul in association with Association of Community Workers.

Gallacher, J., Ohri, A. and Roberts, L. (1983). 'Unemployment and Community Action' in *Community Development Journal*, 18(1): 2–9.

Gamble, A. (1987). 'The Weakening of Social Democracy' in Loney, M., Bocock, R., Clarke, J., Cochrane, A., Graham, P. and Wilson, M. (eds), *The State or the Market: Politics and Welfare in Contemporary Britain*. London: Sage/Open University Press.

Genders, E. and Player, E. (1990). *Race Relations in Prisons*. Oxford: Clarendon Press.

George, V. and Wilding, P. (1985). *Ideology and Social Welfare*. London: Routledge & Kegan Paul.

Giarchi, G.G. (1994). 'The Case for Rural Community Work' in Jacobs, S. and Popple, K. (eds), *Community Work in the 1990's*. Nottingham: Spokesman.

Gilroy, P. (1987). *There Ain't No Black in the Union Jack. The Cultural Politics of Race and Nation*. London: Hutchinson.

Glenn, A. (1993). *A Survey of Community Practitioners in Bradford*. Papers in Community Studies No. 5. Centre for Research in Applied Community Studies. Bradford: Bradford and Ilkley Community College Corporation.

Goetschius, G. (1969). *Working with Community Groups*. London: Routledge & Kegan Paul.

Goetschius, G. (1975). 'Some Difficulties in Introducing a Community Work Option into Social Work Training' in Jones, D. and Mayo, M. (eds), *Community Work Two*, London: Routledge & Kegan Paul.

Goffman, E. (1961). *Asylums*. New York: Doubleday.

Golding, P. and Sills, A. (1983). 'Community against Itself: Social Communication in the Urban Community', *COMM*, 20, December: 177–94. Marcinelle, Belgium: Inter-University European Institute of Social Welfare, rue du Debarcadère 179, B-6001 Marcinelle.

Goodwin, M. and Duncan, S. (1986). 'The Local State and Local Economic Policy: Political Mobilisation or Economic Regeneration' in *Capital and Class*, 27, Winter: 14–36.

Gordon, P. (1989). 'Citizenship for Some? Race and Government Policy 1979–1989', *Runnymede Commentary No. 2*, April. London: Runnymede Trust.

Gough, I. (1979). *The Political Economy of the Welfare State*. London: Macmillan.

Goulbourne, H. (1987). 'West Indian Groups and British Politics', paper presented to the Conference on Black People and British Politics, University of Warwick, November.

Goulbourne, H.D. (ed.) (1990). *Black Politics in Britain*. Aldershot: Avebury.

Gramsci, A. (1971). *Selections from the Prison Notebooks* (edited and translated by Q. Hoare and G. Nowell Smith). London: Lawrence and Wishart.

Gramsci, A. (1975). *Letters from Prison* (selected and translated by J. Lawner). London: Jonathan Cape.

Gramsci, A. (1977). *Selections from Political Writings 1910–1920* (edited by Q. Hoare). London: Lawrence and Wishart.

Gramsci, A. (1978). *Selections from Political Writings 1921–1926* (edited by Q. Hoare). London: Lawrence and Wishart.

Grant, D. (1989). *Learning Relations*. London: Routledge.

Green J. (1992). 'The Community Project Revisited' in Carter, P., Jeffs, T. and Smith, M.K. (eds), *Changing Social Work and Welfare*. Buckingham: Open University Press.

Green, J. and Chapman, A. (1990). 'The Lessons of the CDP for Community Development Today', delivered at the OU/HEC Winter School: 'Roots and Branches: Community Development and Health'.

Griffiths, Sir Roy (1988). *Community Care: Agenda for Action*. London: HMSO.

HMSO (1954). *Social Development in the British Colonial Territories*. Report of the Ashbridge Conference on Social Development (Colonial Office), 3–12 August. London: HMSO.

HMSO (1968). *Report of the Committee on Local Authority and Applied Personal Social Services*, Cmnd. 3703 (Seebohm Report). London: HMSO.

HMSO (1969). *People and Planning* (Skeffington Report). London: HMSO.

HMSO (1981). *The Brixton Disorders 10–12 April 1981: Report of an Inquiry by the Rt. Hon. the Lord Scarman, OBE*, Cmnd. 8427 (Scarman Report). London: HMSO.

HMSO (1986). *Working Together – Education and Training*. London: HMSO.

HMSO (1988). *Mortality Statistics: 1985*. London: HMSO.

HM Treasury (1987). *Treasury Report*. London: HMSO.

Hadley, R. and Hatch, S. (1981). *Social Welfare and the Failure of the State: Centralised Social Services and Participation*. London: Allen & Unwin.

Hadley, R. and McGrath, M. (1980). *Going Local: Neighbourhood and Social Services*. London: Bedford Square Press.

Hadley, R., Cooper, M., Dale, P. and Stacey, G. (1987). *A Community Social Worker's Handbook*. London: Tavistock.

Hall, S. (1988). *The Hard Road to Renewal: Thatcherism and the Crisis of the Left*. London: Verso.

Hall, S. and Jacques, M. (eds) (1989). *New Times: The Changing Face of Politics in the 1990s*. London: Lawrence & Wishart.

Halpern, M. (1963). *The Politics of Social Change in the Middle East and North Africa*. Princeton, New Jersey: Princeton University Press.

Halsey, A.H. (ed.) (1972). *Educational Priority*. London: HMSO.

Hampton, W. (1991). *Local Government and Urban Politics* (2nd edn). Harlow: Longman.

Hanmer, J. and Maynard, M. (1987). *Women, Violence and Social Control*. Basingstoke: Macmillan.

Hanmer, J. and Rose, H. (1980). 'Making Sense of Theory' in Henderson, P., Jones, D. and Thomas, D.N. (eds), *The Boundaries of Change in Community Work*. London: Allen & Unwin.

Hanmer, J. and Statham, D. (1988). *Women and Social Work: Towards a Woman-Centred Practice*. Basingstoke: Macmillan.

Hannington, W. (1967). *Never on Our Knees*. London: Lawrence & Wishart.

Hannington, W. (1977). *Unemployed Struggles: 1919–1936*. London: Lawrence & Wishart.

Hanson, D. (1972). 'Community Centres and their Functions as Educational Institutions and Agencies for Social Control', *Durham Review*, 28.

Harford, B. and Hopkins, S. (eds) (1984). *Greenham Common: Women and the Wire*. London: Women's Press.

Harris, J. (1977). *William Beveridge: A Biography*. Oxford: Clarendon Press.

Harris, J. (1981). 'Social Policy Making in Britain during the Second World War' in

Mommsen, W. (ed.), *The Emergence of the Welfare State in Britain and Germany*. London: Croom Helm.

Harris, L. (1988). 'The UK Economy at a Crossroads' in Allen, J. and Massey, D. (eds), *The Economy in Question*. London: Sage.

Harris, V. (ed.) (1994). *Community Workers' Skills Manual*. Newcastle upon Tyne: Association of Community Workers.

Harvey, B. (1992). *Networking in Europe: A Guide to European Voluntary Organisations*. London: National Council for Voluntary Organisations and the Community Development Foundation.

Heginbotham, C. (1990). *Return to the Community: The Voluntary Ethic and Community Care*. London: Bedford Square Press.

Henderson, P. (1983). 'The Contribution of CDP to the Development of Community Work' in Thomas, D.N. (ed.), *Community Work in the Eighties*. London: National Institute for Social Work.

Henderson, P. and Francis, D. (eds) (1992). *Rural Action – A Collection of Community Work Case Studies*. London: Pluto Press in association with ACRE/CDF.

Henderson, P. and Thomas, D.N. (1987). *Skills in Neighbourhood Work* (2nd edn). London: Allen & Unwin.

Henderson, P., Wright, A. and Wyncoll, K. (eds) (1982). *Successes and Struggles on Council Estates: Tenant Action and Community Work*. London: Association of Community Workers.

Hetherington, P. (1992). 'The Urban Horror on our Doorstep', *Guardian*, 11 July.

Hill, G. (1987). 'Community Work and the MSC', *Talking Point*, no. 85, July. Newcastle upon Tyne: Association of Community Workers.

Hiro, D. (1992). *Black British, White British: A History of Race Relations in Britain*. London: Paladin.

Hobsbawm, E.J. (1968). 'Poverty' in Sills, D.L. (ed.), *New International Encyclopaedia of the Social Sciences*, Vol. 12. London: Macmillan.

Hodge, M. (1987). 'Central–Local Conflicts: The View from Islington' in Hoggett, P. and Hambleton, R. (eds), *Decentralisation and Democracy: Localising Public Services*. Bristol: School for Advanced Urban Studies, University of Bristol.

Hoggett, P. and Hambleton, R. (eds) (1987). *Decentralisation and Democracy: Localising Public Services*. Bristol: School for Advanced Urban Studies, University of Bristol.

Holloway, C. and Otto, S. (1988). *Getting Organized: A Handbook for Non-statutory Organisations*. London: National Council for Voluntary Organisations.

Holmes, J. (1988). 'In Defence of Initial Training', *Youth and Policy*, 23: 1–4.

Home Office (1960). *Children and Young Persons* (Ingleby Report). London: HMSO.

Howard, M. (1993). Letter to Jack Straw MP, 18 November.

Hutson, S. and Liddiard, M. (1994) *Youth Homelessness: the Construction of a Social Issue*. Basingstoke: Macmillan.

Hutton, W. (1993). 'Slouching towards a Recovery', *Guardian*, 18 March.

Iliffe, S. (1985). 'The Politics of Health Care: The NHS under Thatcher', *Critical Social Policy*, 14: 57–72.

Issitt, M. and Woodward, M. (1992). 'Competence and Contradiction' in Carter, P., Jeffs, T. and Smith, M.K. (eds), *Changing Social Work and Welfare*. Buckingham: Open University Press.

Jacobs, B. (1986). *Black Politics and the Urban Crisis in Britain*. Cambridge: Cambridge University Press.

Jacobs, S. (1984). 'Community Action and the Building of Socialism from Below: A Defence of the Non-directive Approach'. *Community Development Journal*, 19(4): 217–24.

Jacobs, S. (1994). 'Community Work in a Changing World' in Jacobs, S. and Popple, K. (eds), *Community Work in the 1990s*. Nottingham: Spokesman.

James, J. (1990). 'Public Services and the Black Community' in Schofield, A. (ed.), *Report of the Social Work Education and Racism Workshop 29th–30th March 1990 at Ruskin College*. Oxford: Community Education Research and Training Unit, Ruskin College.

Jeffs, A.J. (1979). *Young People and the Youth Service*. London: Routledge & Kegan Paul.

Jeffs, T. and Smith, M. (1990). 'Young People, Class Inequality and Youth Work' in Jeffs, T. and Smith, M. (eds), *Young People, Inequality and Youth Work*. Basingstoke: Macmillan Education.

Jessup, G. (1990). 'National Vocational Qualifications: Implications for Further Education' in Bees, M. and Swords, M. (eds), *National Vocational Qualifications and Further Education*. London: Kogan Page.

John, G. (1981). *In the Service of Black Youth: The Political Culture of Youth and Community Work with Black People in English Cities*. Leicester: National Association of Youth Clubs.

Johnson, C. (1991). *The Economy under Mrs Thatcher 1979–1990*. London: Penguin Books.

Jones, D. (1977). 'Community Work in the United Kingdom' in Specht, H. and Vickery, A. (eds), *Integrating Social Work Methods*. London: Allen & Unwin.

Jones, D. (1983). 'Community of Interest: A Reprise' in Thomas, D.N. (ed.), *Community Work in the Eighties*. London: National Institute of Social Work.

Jones, D. and Mayo, M. (eds) (1975). *Community Work Two*. London: Routledge & Kegan Paul.

Jones, G.S. (1976). *Outcast London*. Harmondsworth: Penguin.

Jones, K. and Fowles, A.J. (1984). *Ideas on Institutions*. London: Routledge & Kegan Paul.

Jones, L. (1986). 'The Community Programme Scheme', *Talking Point*, no. 77, October. Newcastle upon Tyne: Association of Community Workers.

Joseph, K. (1972). 'The Next Ten Years', *New Society*, 5 October.

Kalka, I. (1991). 'The Politics of the "Community" among Gujarati Hindus in London', *New Community*, 17(3): 377–85.

Kelly, L. (1988). *Surviving Sexual Violence*. Cambridge: Polity Press.

Kettle, M. (1988). 'Years of Revolution' in *68/88*. London: Channel 4 Television.

Kinder, C. (1985). *Community Start-up: How To Start a Community Group and Keep it Going*. London: National Federation of Community Organisations.

Kramer, R. (1979). 'Voluntary Agencies in the Welfare State: An Analysis of the Vanguard Role', *Journal of Social Policy*, 8(4): 473–88.

Kuenstler, P. (1961). *Community Organisations in Great Britain*. London: Faber.

Kuper, B. (1985). 'The Supply of Training', *Youth and Policy*, 13, Summer: 15–18.

Kwo, E.M. (1984). 'Community Education and Community Development in Cameroon: The British Colonial Experience, 1922–1961', *Community Development Journal*, 19(4): 204–13.

Lamoureux, H., Mayer, R. and Panet-Raymond, J. (1989). *Community Action*. Quebec: Black Rose Books.

Land, H. (1980). 'The Family Wage', *Feminist Review*, 6: 55–77.

Langan, M. (1990). 'Community Care in the 1990s – The Community Care White Paper: "Caring for People"', *Critical Social Policy*, 29, Autumn: 58–70.

Lapping, A. (ed.) (1970). *Community Action* (Fabian Tract 400). London: Fabian Society.

Laurence, S. and Hall, P. (1981). 'British Policy Responses' in Hall, P. (ed.), *The Inner City in Context. The Final Report of the Social Science Research Council Inner Cities Working Party*. Aldershot: Gower.

Leaper, R.A.B. (1971). *Community Work*. London: National Council of Social Service.

Leat, D. (1988). *Voluntary Organisations and Accountability*. London: National Council for Voluntary Organisations.

Leavitas, R. (ed.) (1986). *The Ideology of the New Right*. Cambridge: Polity Press.

Lee, B. and Weeks, W. (1991). 'Social Action Theory and the Women's Movement: An Analysis of Assumption', *Community Development Journal*, 26(3): 220–26.

Lees, R. and Mayo, M. (1984). *Community Action for Change*. London: Routledge & Kegan Paul.

Leicester Outwork Campaign (1987). *Leicester Outwork Campaign Annual Report 1986–87*. Leicester: Leicester Outwork Campaign, 132 Regent Road, Leicester LE1 7PA.

Leissner, A. (1984). *Community Work: Guidelines and Models for Students, Field Supervisors and Practitioners* (4th edn). Keele: University of Keele.

Leonard, P. (ed.) (1975). *The Sociology of Community Action*, Sociological Review Monograph 21. Keele: University of Keele.

Lewis, J. (1986). 'Feminism and Welfare' in Mitchell, J. and Oakley, A. (eds), *What is Feminism?* Oxford: Basil Blackwell.

Lewis, J. and Meredith, B. (1990). *Daughters Who Care*. London: Routledge.

Lewycka, M. (1986). 'The Way They Were', *New Socialist*, 36, March: 16–18.

Linebaugh, P. (1982). 'All the Atlantic Mountains Shook', *Labour/Le Travail*, 10, Autumn.

Linebaugh, P. (1984). 'Reply to Sweeny', *Labour/Le Travail*, 14, Autumn.

London Edinburgh Weekend Return Group (1980). *In and Against the State*. London: Pluto Press.

Loney, M. (1983). *Community against Government: The British Community Development Project 1968–78*. London: Heinemann Educational Books.

Loney, M., Bocock, R., Clarke, J., Cochrane, A., Graham, P. and Wilson, M. (eds) (1991). *The State or the Market: Politics and Welfare in Contemporary Britain*. (Second Edition). London: Sage in association with Open University Press.

Loudon, J.B. (1961). 'Kinship and Crisis in South Wales', *British Journal of Sociology*, XII(4): 333–40.

Lovett, T. (1975). *Adult Education, Community Development and the Working Class*. London: Ward Lock.

Lovett, T., Clarke, C. and Kilmurray, A. (1983). *Adult Education and Community Action*. London: Croom Helm.

Lowe, J. (1973). *The Managers. A Survey of Youth Club Management*. London: Inner London Education Authority.

Lowe, S. (1986). *Urban Social Movements*. London: Macmillan Education.

McConnell, C. (1992). *Promoting Community Development in Europe*. London: Community Development Foundation.

McCrindle, J. and Rowbotham, S. (1986). 'More Than Just a Memory', *Feminist Review*, 23, Summer: 109–24.

McDermott, K. (1990). 'We Have No Problem: The Experience of Racism in Prison', *New Community*, 16(2): 213–28.

McIntosh, M. (1981). 'Feminism and Social Policy', *Critical Social Policy*, 1: 32–42.

McKay, D. and Cox, A. (1979). *The Politics of Urban Change*. London: Croom Helm.

McLeod, E. (1982). *Women Working: Prostitution Now*. London: Croom Helm.

McMichael, P., Lynch, B. and Wright, D. (1990). *Building Bridges into Work: The Role of the Community Worker*. Harlow: Longman.

McNeil, S. and Rhodes, D. (eds) (1985). *Women against Violence against Women*. London: Only Women Press.

Malos, E. (1980). *The Politics of Housework*. London: Allen & Busby.

Mama, A. (1989). *The Hidden Struggle: Statutory and Voluntary Responses to Violence against Black Women in the Home*. London: London Race and Housing Unit.

Marris, P. (1987). *Meaning and Action: Planning and Conceptions of Change*. London: Routledge & Kegan Paul.

Marsden, D. and Oakley, P. (1982). 'Radical Community Development in the Third

World' in Craig, G., Derricourt, N. and Loney, M. (eds). *Community Work and the State: Community Work Eight*. London: Routledge & Kegan Paul.

Marshall, T.H. (1975). *Social Policy*. London: Hutchinson.

Martin, I. (1987). 'Community Education: Towards a Theoretical Analysis' in Allen, G., Bastiani, J., Martin, I. and Richards, K. (eds), *Community Education: An Agenda for Educational Reform*. Milton Keynes: Open University Press.

Martin, R. (1987). *Being White: A Training Video*. London: Albany Video Distribution, The Albany, Douglas Way, London SE8 4AG.

Mayo, M. (1975). 'The History and Early Development of CDP' in Lees, R. and Smith, G. (eds), *Action Research in Community Development*. London: Routledge & Kegan Paul.

Mayo, M. (ed.) (1977). *Women in the Community. Community Work Three*. London: Routledge & Kegan Paul.

Mayo, M. (1980). 'Beyond CDP: reaction and community action' in Bailey, R. and Brake, M. (eds), *Radical Social Work and Practice*. London: Edward Arnold.

Mayo, M. (1982). 'Community Action Programmes in the Early Eighties – What Future?', *Critical Social Policy*, 1(3): 5–18.

Mayo, M. (1994). *Communities and Caring: The Mixed Economy of Welfare*. Basingstoke: Macmillan.

Mayo, M. and Jones, D. (eds) (1974). *Community Work One*. London: Routledge & Kegan Paul.

Meier, P. (1978). *William Morris: The Marxist Dreamer* (translated by F. Gubb). Brighton: Harvester.

Melling, J. (1980). 'Clydeside Housing and the Evolution of State Rent Control' in Melling, J. (ed.), *Housing, Social Policy and the State*. London: Croom Helm.

Midwinter, E. (1972). *Priority Education*. Harmondsworth: Penguin.

Midwinter, E. (1975). *Education and the Community*. London: George Allen & Unwin.

Millar, J. (1987). *You Can't Kill the Spirit*. London: Women's Press.

Millet, K. (1969). *Sexual Politics*. London: Abacus.

Mills, R. (1983). 'Trusts and Foundations as Innovative Bodies' in Thomas, D.N. (ed.), *Community Work in the Eighties*. London: National Institute for Social Work.

Moore, B. (1992). 'Taking on the Inner Cities' in Michie, J. (ed.), *The Economic Legacy 1979–1992*. London: Academic Press.

Morris, H. (1925). *The Village College: Being a Memorandum on the Provision of Educational and Social Facilities for the Countryside, with Special Reference to Cambridgeshire*. Cambridge: Cambridge University Press.

Morris, J. (1990). *Pride without Prejudice*. London: Women's Press.

Morris, P. (1969). *Put Away: A Sociological Study of Institutions for the Mentally Retarded*. London: Routledge & Kegan Paul.

Morris, W. (1887). 'The Society of the Future' in Morton, A.R. (ed.), *Political Writings*. London: Lawrence & Wishart.

Morris, W. (1918). *A Dream of John Ball*. London: Longmans.

Morrison, C. (1984). *Howgill: Developing Work in the Community*. London: Save the Children Fund.

Mowatt, C.L. (1955). *Britain between the Wars*. London: Methuen.

Mowatt, C.L. (1961). *The Charity Organisation Society, 1869–1913: Its Ideas and Work*. London: Methuen.

Mullard, C. (1973). *Black Britain*. London: Allen & Unwin.

Mullard, C. (1984). *Anti-Racist Education: The Three O's*. Cardiff: National Antiracist Movement in Education.

Munday, B. (1980). 'The Permeation of Community Work into Other Disciplines' in Henderson, P. Jones, D. and Thomas, D.N. (eds), *The Boundaries of Change in Community Work*. London: Allen & Unwin.

Nathan, Lord (1990). *Effectiveness and the Voluntary Sector*. London: National Council for Voluntary Organisations.

National Association for the Care and Resettlement of Offenders (1988). *Some Facts and Findings about Black People in the Criminal Justice System*. London: National Association for the Care and Resettlement of Offenders.

National Association of Probation Officers (1988). *Racism, Representation and the Criminal Justice System*. London: National Association of Probation Officers.

National Council for Voluntary Organisations (1988). *Releasing Enterprise, Voluntary Organisations and the Inner City*. London: National Council for Voluntary Organisations/Bedford Square Press.

National Child Care Campaign (1985). *National Childcare Campaign Policy Statement*. London: National Child Care Campaign.

National Council for Voluntary Organisations (1991). *The Voluntary Agencies Directory*. London: National Council for Voluntary Organisations/Bedford Square Press.

Newham Docklands Forum and Greater London Council Popular Planning Unit (1983). *People's Plan for the Royal Docks*. London: Greater London Council.

Ng, R. (1988). *The Politics of Community Services: Immigrant Women, Class and the State*. Toronto: Garamond Press.

Ohri, A., Manning, B. and Curno, P. (eds) (1982). *Community Work and Racism: Community Work Seven*. London: Routledge & Kegan Paul in association with the Association of Community Workers.

Ohri, A. and Roberts, L. (1981). 'Can Community Workers Do Anything about Unemployment?', *Talking Point*, no. 28. London: Association of Community Workers.

O'Malley, J. (1977). *Politics of Community Action*. London: Russell.

OPCS (1993a). *1991 Census: Report for Great Britain*. Office of Population Censuses and Surveys. London: HMSO.

OPCS (1993b). *1991 Census: Report for Greater London*. Office of Population Censuses and Surveys. London: HMSO.

Pahl, J. (ed.) (1985a). *Private Violence and Public Policy: The Needs of Battered Women and the Response of the Public Services*. London: Routledge & Kegan Paul.

Pahl, J. (1985b). 'Refuges for Battered Women: Ideology and Action', *Feminist Review*, 19, Spring: 25–43.

Pahl, R.E. (1966). The Rural–Urban Continuum, *Sociologia Ruralis*, 6: 299–329.

Parker, R.A. (1981). 'Tending and Social Policy' in Goldberg, E.M. and Hatch, S. (eds), *A New Look at the Personal Social Services*. London: Policy Studies Institute.

Parr, J. (1991). *Student Discretionary Awards (Intake) Survey 1977–1990 Inclusive*. Birmingham: Westhill College.

Parry, N. and Parry, J. (1979). 'Social Work, Professionalism and the State' in Parry, N., Rustin, M. and Satyamurti, C. (eds), *Social Work, Welfare and the State*. London: Edward Arnold.

Pascall, G. (1986). *Social Policy: A Feminist Analysis*. London: Tavistock.

Pearse, M. and Smith, J. (1990). *Community Groups Handbook*. London: Journeyman Press/Community Development Foundation.

Pearson, G. (1983). *Hooligan: A History of Respectable Fears*. London: Macmillan.

Peatfield, P. (1992). *The Only Step in the Line: The Lone Manager in the Small Voluntary Organisation*. London: Centre for Voluntary Organisations.

Phillips, M. (1989). 'Kent Takes the Fast Line to Rebellion', *Guardian*, 22 February.

Pickvance, C. (1977). 'Marxist Approaches to the Study of Urban Politics', *International Journal of Urban and Regional Research*, 1: 218–55.

Piven, F. and Cloward, R. (1977). *Poor People's Movement: Why They Succeed, How They Fail*. New York: Vintage Books.

Popple, K. (1990). 'Youth Work and Race' in Jeffs, T. and Smith, M. (eds), *Young People, Inequality and Youth Work*. London: Macmillan.

Popple, K. (1994). 'Towards a Progressive Community Work Praxis' in Jacobs, S. and Popple, K. (eds), *Community Work in the 1990's*. Nottingham: Spokesman.

Powell, E. (1968). 'Text of Speech Delivered in Birmingham, 20 April 1968', *Race*, X(1): 80–104.

Purcell, R. (1982). 'Community Action and Real Work', *Talking Point*, No. 32. London: Association of Community Workers.

Pye, A. (1991). 'Management Competence: "The Flower in the Mirror and the Moon on the Water"' in Silver, H. (ed.), *Competent to Manage*. London: Routledge.

Radford, J. (1970). 'From King Hill to the Squatting Association' in Lapping, A. (ed.), *Community Action* (Fabian Tract 400). London: Fabian Society.

Redman, W. and Rogers, A. (1988). *Show What You Know: Helping Youth and Community Workers Build a Portfolio of Their Experience and Learning*. Leicester: National Youth Bureau.

Rée, H. (1973). *Educator Extraordinary: The Life and Achievements of Henry Morris*. London: Longman.

Rée, H. (1985). *The Henry Morris Collection*. Cambridge: Cambridge University Press.

Richardson, A. (1984). *Working with Self-Help Groups: A Guide for Local Professionals*. London: Bedford Square Press/National Council for Voluntary Organisations.

Ridley, N. (1988). *The Local Right: Enabling Not Providing*. London: Centre for Policy Studies.

Rimmer, J. (1980). *Troubles Shared: The Story of a Settlement 1899–1979*. Birmingham: Phlogiston.

Robb, B. (ed.) (1967). *Sans Everything: A Case to Answer*. London: Nelson.

Roberts, H. (ed.) (1982). *Women's Health Matters*. London: Routledge.

Roberts, L. (1992). 'A Community Development Perspective on Community Care', *Talking Point*, no. 132. Newcastle upon Tyne: Association of Community Workers.

Robertson, C. (1991). 'Moral Trust Comes before Skills and Information Technology', *Talking Point*, no. 122. Newcastle upon Tyne: Association of Community Workers.

Robertson, D. (1985). *The Penguin Dictionary of Politics*. London: Penguin.

Rogers, R. (1990). *Managing Consultancy: A Guide for Arts and Voluntary Organisations*. London: National Council for Voluntary Organisations.

Rogers, V. (1994). 'Feminist Work and Community Education' in Jacobs, S. and Popple, K. (eds), *Community Work in the 1990s*. Nottingham: Spokesman.

Roof (1986). 'The Penny Drops at Coin Street', *Roof*, March/April: 6–7.

Rosenberg, J.D. (1961). *The Darkening Glass*. New York: Columbia University Press.

Ross, M. (1955). *Community Organisation*. Theory, Principles and Practice. New York: Harper and Row.

Rothman, J. (1970). 'Three Models of Community Organisation Practice' in Cox, F., Erlich, J., Rothman, J. and Tropman, J. (eds), *Strategies of Community Organisation*. Itaska, Illinois: Peacock Publishing.

Rowbotham, S. (1977). *Hidden from History*. London: Pluto Press.

Rowbotham, S. (1979). 'Women: How Far Have We Come?', *Hackney People's Press*, November; reprinted in Rowbotham, S. (1983), *Dreams and Dilemmas*. London: Virago.

Rowbotham, S. (1989). *The Past is before Us: Feminism in Action since the 1960s*. London: Penguin.

Rowbotham, S. (1992). *Women in Movement: Feminism and Social Action*. London: Routledge.

Runnymede Trust (1992). *Race and Immigration*. Bulletin 251. London: Runnymede Trust.

Ruzek, S. (1986). 'Feminist Visions of Health: An International Perspective' in Mitchell, J. and Oakley, A. (eds), *What is Feminism?* Oxford: Basil Blackwell.

Scottish Council for Community and Voluntary Organisations (1984). *The Garnock Valley Community Project: Final Report.* Edinburgh: Scottish Council for Community and Voluntary Organisations.

Salmon, H. (1984). *Unemployment: The Two Nations.* London: Association of Community Workers.

Sapin, K. (1989). *The Community Work Accreditation Process: The Pilot in Greater Manchester.* Manchester: Greater Manchester Community Work Training Group.

Saunders, P. (1983). *Urban Politics: A Sociological Interpretation.* London: Hutchinson.

Sayer, J. (1986). 'Ideology: The Bridge between Theory and Practice', *Community Development Journal*, 21(4): 294–303.

Scase, R. (1992). *Class.* Buckingham: Open University Press.

Schumpeter, J. (1976). *Capitalism, Socialism and Democracy* (first published 1942). London: Allen & Unwin.

Scott, A. (1990). *Ideology and the New Social Movements.* London: Unwin Hyman.

Scott, D. (1990). *Positive Perspectives: Developing the Contribution of Unqualified Workers in Community and Youth Work.* Harlow: Longman.

Scull, A.T. (1977). *Decarceration: Community Treatment and the Deviant: A Radical View.* Englewood Cliffs, New Jersey: Prentice Hall.

Seddon, V. (1986). *The Cutting Edge: Women and the Pit Strike.* London: Lawrence & Wishart.

Seed, P. (1973). *The Expansion of Social Work in Great Britain.* London: Routledge & Kegan Paul.

Segal, L. (1990). 'Pornography and Violence: What the "Experts" Really Say', *Feminist Review*, 36, Autumn: 29–41.

Silburn, R. (1971). 'The Potential and Limitations of Community Action' in Bull, D. (ed.), *Family Poverty.* London: Duckworth & Co.

Simon, R. (1982). *Gramsci's Political Thought.* London: Lawrence & Wishart.

Sinclair, T. (1987). 'Apprenticeship Training', *Youth and Policy*, 21, Summer: 21–7.

Sivanandan, A. (1976). *Race, Class and the State.* London: Institute of Race Relations.

Sivanandan, A. (1990). *Communities of Resistance: Writings on Black Struggles for Socialism.* London: Verso.

Sked, A. and Cook, C. (1984). *Post-War Britain: A Political History* (2nd edn). London: Penguin.

Smith, I. (1980). 'Community Work and "Qualifications"', *Talking Point*, no. 19. London: Association of Community Workers.

Smith, I. (1989). 'Community Work in Recession: A Practioner's Perspective' in Langan, M. and Lee, P. (eds), *Radical Social Work Today.* London: Unwin Hyman.

Smith, L. and Jones, D. (eds) (1981). *Deprivation, Participation and Communication Action. Community Work Six.* London: Routledge & Kegan Paul.

Smith, M. (1979). 'Concepts of Community Work: A British View', in Chekki, D.A. (ed.), *Community Development: Theory and Method of Manned Change.* New Delhi: Vika Publishing House.

Smithies, J. and Webster, G. (1987). 'Feminist Organising and Community Work: A Response to Hilary Barker, "Recapturing Sisterhood" in *Critical Social Policy*, Issue 16', *Critical Social Policy*, 20: 83–85.

Solomos, J. (1989). *Black Youth, Racism and the State: The Politics of Ideology and Policy.* Cambridge: Cambridge University Press.

Sondhi, R. (1982). 'The Asian Resource Centre' in Cheetham, J. (ed.), *Ethnicity and Social Work.* Oxford: Oxford University Press.

Sondhi, R. (1994). 'From Black British to Black European: A Crisis of Identity' in Jacobs, S. and Popple, K. (eds), *Community Work in the 1990s.* Nottingham: Spokesman.

Spence, J. (1985). 'Unemployment, Youth and National Community Service', *Youth and Policy*, 13, Summer: 6–11.

Stacey, M. (1969). 'The Myth of Community Studies', *British Journal of Sociology*. 20: 134–47.

Stanley, L. and Wise, S. (1983). *Breaking Out. Feminist Consciousness and Feminist Research*. London: Routledge & Kegan Paul.

Stanton, A. (1989). *Invitation to Self Management*. Ruislip: Dab Hand Press.

Stevenson, J. and Cook, C. (1977). *The Slump: Society and Politics during the Depression*. London: Cape.

Tasker, L. (1980). 'Practice and Theory in Community Work: A Case for Reconciliation' in Henderson, P., Jones, D. and Thomas, D.N. (eds). *The Boundaries of Change in Community Work*. London: Allen & Unwin.

Taylor, A.J.P. (1965). *English History 1914–1945*. Oxford: Oxford University Press.

Taylor, M. (1979). 'Managing Community Resources', *Talking Point*, no. 13. London: Association of Community Workers.

Taylor, M. (1983). *Inside a Community Project: Bedworth Heath*. London: Community Projects Foundation.

Taylor, M. (1992). *Signposts to Community Development*. London: Community Development Foundation and the National Coalition of Neighbourhoods.

Taylor, M. and Presley, F. (1987). *Community Work in the UK 1982–6* (edited by Chanan, G.). London: Library Association Publishing in association with Calouste Gulbenkian Foundation.

Thane, P. (1989). *Foundations of the Welfare State*. London: Longman.

Thomas, D.N. (1978). 'Community Work, Social Change and Social Planning' in Curno, P. (ed.), *Political Issues and Community Work*. London: Routledge & Kegan Paul.

Thomas, D.N. (1980). 'Research and Community Work', *Community Development Journal*, 15(1): 30–40.

Thomas, D.N. (1983). *The Making of Community Work*. London: George Allen & Unwin.

Thompson, E.P. (1977). *William Morris – From Romantic to Revolutionary*. London: Merlin.

Thorns, D.C. (1976). *The Quest for Community: Social Aspects of Residential Growth*. London: George Allen & Unwin.

Tönnies, F. (1955). *Community and Association*. London: Routledge & Kegan Paul.

Townsend, P. (1962). *The Last Refuge: A Survey of Residential Institutions and Homes for the Aged in England and Wales*. London: Routledge & Kegan Paul.

Troyna, B. (1987). 'Beyond Multi-culturalism: Towards the Enactment of Anti-racist Education in Policy, Provision and Pedagogy'. *Oxford Review of Education*, 13(3): 307–20.

Troyna, B. and Carrington, B. (1990). *Education, Racism and Reform*. London: Routledge.

Twelvetrees, A. (1976). *Community Associations and Centres: A Comparative Study*. Oxford: Pergamon.

Twelvetrees, A. (1983). 'Whither Community Work?' in Thomas D.N. (ed.), *Community Work in the Eighties*. London: National Institute for Social Work.

Twelvetrees, A. (1991). *Community Work* (2nd edn). London: Macmillan.

Twelvetrees, A. and Shuttleworth, D. (1985). 'Community Development Corporations: Lessons for the UK', *Initiatives*, 2, December.

United Nations (1959). *European Seminar on Community Development and Social Welfare in Urban Areas*. Geneva: United Nations.

Unemployment Unit and Youth Aid (1993). *Working Brief*, February/March. London: Unemployment Unit and Youth Aid.

Ungerson, C. (1987). *Policy is Personal*. London: Tavistock.

Vaz, K. (1993). *Sinking Our Cities? The Effects of the Government's Abolition of the Urban Programme*. London: Labour Party.

Vidal, J. (1993). 'And the Eco-feminists Shall Inherit the Earth', *Guardian*, 9 August.

Waddington, D., Wykes, M. and Chritcher, C. (1991). *Split at the Seam? Community, Continuity and Change after the 1984–5 Coal Dispute*. Milton Keynes: Open University Press.

Waddington, P. (1983). 'Looking Ahead – Community Work into the 1980s' in Thomas, D.N. (ed.), *Community Work in the Eighties*. London: National Institute for Social Work.

Wagner, G. (1988). *Residential Care: A Positive Choice*. London: National Institute for Social Work/HMSO.

Walker, A. (1987). 'Introduction: A Policy for Two Nations' in Walker, A. and Walker, C. (eds), *The Growing Divide: A Social Audit 1979–1987*. London: Child Poverty Action Group.

Walker, A. (1989). 'Community Care' in McCarthy, M. (ed.), *The New Politics of Welfare*. Basingstoke: Macmillan Education.

Walton, R.G. (1975). *Women in Social Work*. London: Routledge & Kegan Paul.

Walvin, J. (1985). 'Abolishing the Slave Trade: Anti-slavery and Popular Radicalism, 1776–1807' in Emsley, T. and Walvin, J. (eds), *Artisans, Peasants and Proletarians*. London: Croom Helm.

Ware, V. (1991). *Beyond the Pale: White Women, Racism and History*. London: Verso.

Webb, C. (ed.) (1986). *Feminist Practice in Women's Health Care*. Chichester: Wiley.

Weber, M. (1930). *The Protestant Ethic and the Spirit of Capitalism* (first published in German in 1904–5). London: Allen & Unwin.

Weber, M. (1978). *Economy and Society: An Outline of Interpretive Sociology* (2 vols). Berkley: University of California Press.

Weston, C. (1993). 'Firms to Receive Subsidy on Jobs', *Guardian*, 17 March.

Whitham, J. (1986). *Hearts and Minds*. London: Canary Press.

Whitting, G., Burton, P., Means, R. and Stewart, M. (1986). *The Urban Programme and the Young Unemployed*. Inner Cities Research Programme. London: Department of the Environment.

Wicks, M. (1987). *A Future for All*. Harmondsworth: Penguin.

Williams, R. (1976). *Keywords*. London: Fontana/Croom Helm.

Williams, F. (1989). *Social Policy: A Critical Introduction*. Oxford: Polity Press.

Williamson, H. (1988). 'Youth Workers, the MSC and the Youth Training Scheme' in Jeffs, T. and Smith, M. (eds), *Welfare and Youth Work Practice*. Basingstoke: Macmillan Education.

Wilmott, P. (1963). *The Evolution of a Community*. London: Routledge & Kegan Paul.

Wilmott, P. (1989). *Community Initiatives: Patterns and Prospects*. London: Policy Studies Institute.

Wilmott, P. and Thomas, D. (1984). *Community in Social Policy*. London: Policy Studies Institute.

Wilson, E. (1977). *Women and the Welfare State*. London: Tavistock.

Wilson, E. (1982). 'Women, the "Community" and the "Family"', in Walker, A. (ed.), *Community Care: The Family, the State and Social Policy*. Oxford: Basil Blackwell.

Wilson, E. (1983). 'Feminism and Social Policy' in Loney, M., Boswell, D. and Clarke, J. (eds), *Social Policy and Social Welfare*. Milton Keynes: Open University Press.

Wilson, E. with Weir, A. (1986). *Hidden Agendas: Theory, Politics and Experience in the Women's Movement*. London: Tavistock.

Younghusband, E.L. (1959). *Report of the Working Party on Social Workers in the Local Authority Health and Welfare Services*. London: HMSO.

Yurval, D. (1992). 'Fundamentalism, Multiculturalism and Women in Britain' in Donald, J. and Rattansi, A. (eds). *'Race', Culture and Difference*. London: Sage/Open University Press.

Appendix *A*

SELECT COMMUNITY
DEVELOPMENT PROJECT
BIBLIOGRAPHY

Benwell CDP (1978). *Slums on the Drawing Board, Final Report No. 4*. Newcastle: Benwell CDP.

Birmingham CDP (1987). *Youth on the Dole, Final Report No. 4*. Birmingham and Oxford: Birmingham CDP Research Team and the Social Evaluation Unit, Oxford University.

Birmingham CDP (1978). *Leasehold Loopholes, Final Report No. 5*. Birmingham and Oxford: Birmingham CDP Research Team and the Social Evaluation Unit, Oxford University.

Butterworth, E., Lees, R. and Arnold, P. (1980). *The Challenge of Community Work, Final Report of Batley CDP, Papers in Community Studies, No. 24*. York: University of York.

Canning Town CDP (1975a). *Canning Town to North Woolwich: The Aims of Industry?* London: Canning Town CDP.

Canning Town CDP (1975b). *Canning Town's Declining Community Income*. London: Canning Town CDP.

Canning Town CDP (1976). *Growth and Decline: Canning Town's Economy 1846–1946*. London: Canning Town CDP.

CDP (1977a). *Gilding the Ghetto, The State and The Poverty Experiments*. London: Community Development Project Inter-project Editorial Team.

CDP (1977b). *The Costs of Industrial Change*. London: Community Development Project and Inter-project Editorial Team.

CDP IIU (1975). *The Poverty of the Improvement Programme*. London: CDP Information and Intelligence Unit.

CDP IIU (1976a). *Profits against Houses*. London: CDP Information and Intelligence Unit.

CDP IIU (1976b). *Whatever Happened to Council Housing?* London: CDP Information and Intelligence Unit.

CDP PEC (1979). *The State and the Local Economy*. London: CDP PEC and Publications Distributive Co-operative.

CIS/CDP (1976). *Cutting the Welfare State (Who Profits?)*. London: Counter Information Services and CDP.

Corina, L. (1977). *Oldham CDP: An Assessment of its Impact and Influence on the Local Authority, Papers in Community Studies, No. 9*. York: University of York.

Corina, L., Collis, P. and Crosby, C. (1979). *Oldham CDP: The Final Report*. York: University of York.

Coventry CDP (1975a). *Coventry and Hillfields: Prosperity and the Persistence of Inequality, Final Report, Part 1*. Coventry: Coventry CDP.

Coventry CDP (1975b). *Background Working Papers, Final Report, Part 2*. Coventry: Coventry CDP.

North Tyneside CDP (1978a). *North Shields: Working Class Politics and Housing 1900–77, Final Report, Vol. 1*. Newcastle: Newcastle upon Tyne Polytechnic.

North Tyneside CDP (1978b). *North Shields: Organizing for Change in a Working Class Area, Final Report, Vol. 3*. Newcastle: Newcastle upon Tyne Polytechnic.

North Tyneside CDP (1978c). *North Shields: Organizing for Change in A Working Class Area: The Action Groups, Final Report, Vol. 4*. Newcastle: Newcastle upon Tyne Polytechnic.

North Tyneside CDP (1978d). *Women's Work, Final Report, Vol. 5*. Newcastle: Newcastle upon Tyne Polytechnic.

North Tyneside CDP (1978e). *In and Out of Work: A Study of Unemployment, Low Pay and Income Maintenance Services*. Newcastle: Newcastle upon Tyne Polytechnic.

Penn, R. and Alden, J. (1977). *Upper Afan CDP Final Report to Sponsors. Joint Report by Action Team and Research Team Directors, Cardiff, University of Wales, Institute of Science and Technology*. Cardiff: University of Wales.

JOB CATEGORIES WHERE COMMUNITY WORK TRAINING UNITS COULD BE OF RELEVANCE

- Adult basic education tutors
- adult education workers
- advice and information officers
- AIDS workers
- architects
- community arts workers
- community involvement police
- counsellors
- countryside rangers
- curators
- environmental workers
- family centre staff
- health education and promotion workers
- housing development officers
- landscape gardeners
- librarians
- managers at different levels
- outreach workers
- planners
- play and playworkers
- reminiscence staff (working with people to recall the past)
- resource centre staff
- social workers
- sports development officers
- stewards in community centres
- volunteer training organizers

- workers for the Church
- workers involved in housing issues
- workers involved with development of local management
- workers with co-operatives
- workers with tenants' associations
- workers with the under-sevens
- youth workers.

Source: Convention of Scottish Local Authorities (1990).

INDEX

Abrams, P., 2
Alinsky, S., 65
Allen, G., 63
Allman, P., 64
anarchism, 34
Association of Community Workers, 20, 72, 77, 78, 89

Baldock, P., 7
Barclay Report, 26, 59
Barker, H., 68
Barr, A., 61, 93
Batten, R., 14, 33, 60
Bédarida, F., 11, 12
Benfield, G., 6
Benyon, J., 17, 27
Beresford, P., 58
Biddle, L. & W., 33, 60
black and anti-racist community work, 69, 71, 72, 83
  experience of black workers, 75, 77
black consciousness, 8, 38, 70
Boddy, M., 17
Bolger, S., 17, 36
British Association of Settlements and Social Action Centres, 12, 77
Burns, D., 28
Butcher, H., 3, 29, 83, 84, 85

Calouste Gulbenkian Foundation, 14, 20
Campaign for Nuclear Disarmament, 19
Castells, M., 49–50
Chapman, A., 21
Charity Organisation Society, 9
Child Poverty Action Group, 19
City Challenge, 87, 88
Cockburn, C., 3, 22, 65, 67
Cole, G.D.H., 2
community
  black, 3, 71
  and class, 3
  and class struggle, 3
  definition of, 2–4
  and its relationship to the state, 3
community action, 7, 14, 28, 30, 35, 48, 65
  definition of, 65
  role of community worker, 66
Community Action (magazine), 27, 28, 65
community care, 29, 55
  as a community work model, 58, 100
  and the New Right, 58
  and women, 58
community centres, 12
community charge, 28

community college movement, 63
community development, 60–1, 100
  and Europe, 29
Community Development Journal, 20
Community Development Projects, 5,
    15, 16, 18, 19, 21, 40, 44, 63
  critique by feminists and anti-racists, 37
  lack of practice, 36
  theoretical contribution of, 36
Community Education, 62
  definition of, 62
  theoretical influences on, 63
Community Programme, 21, 24, 28
community work
  and the amelioration of dissent, 12,
    19, 27, 40, 46, 101
  and benevolent paternalism, 7, 10, 30
  and central government, 27
  and the church, 10
  and class, 8, 11, 35, 90
  and colonialism, 8, 14
  and community care, 29, 55, 58, 100
  and conflict, 14, 35
  contemporary challenges in, 30
  definition of, 1, 4–5, 83
  as a developmental activity, 4
  as a distributive activity, 4
  and education, 4, 12, 33
  employment and funding of, 83, 87,
    88, 93, 94
  and Europe, 29
  goals, 5, 23, 67
  golden age of, 15, 24
  government intervention in, 12
  history of, 8–13, 14, 34, 97
  and idealism, 19
  and imperialism, 7–8, 60
  influence of benevolent
    paternalism, 7, 10, 30
  influence of black and anti-racist-
    critique, 5, 38, 69–72, 98
  influence of black women, 38
  influence of feminism, 5, 37, 41, 90, 98
  influence of Gramsci, A., 43–6, 101
  influence of Freire, P., 52, 63–4, 101
  influences on other professions, 40
  in rural areas, 5
  in the inner city, 27, 85
  international influences, 14, 15
  and the labour movement, 5, 8, 13,
    36, 65
  and liberation, 40, 46

  and local government, 27, 29
  maintaining the status quo, 12, 19,
    27, 40, 46
  management of, 91, 93, 94
  and Marxism, 3, 35, 40, 41
  models, 55, 58, 60, 61, 62, 99
  and the New Right, 24–6, 58, 97
  non directive approaches in, 14
  as an occupation, 33
  and participation, 32
  pluralist theory, 4, 27, 32, 39, 40, 96,
    97
  as a political activity, 33, 46, 50
  political neutrality in, 27
  practice, 5, 19, 33, 46, 67, 74, 78, 83,
    89, 93
  prefiguring society, 51
  as a profession, 40
  and race, 16, 21, 71
  radical, 4, 18, 41, 98
  radical practice, 5, 34, 98
  role of, 23, 45
  role of the voluntary sector, 12, 13
  self help, 12
  skills, 27, 33, 89, 90
  and social democracy, 13
  and social movements, 46–53, 102
  and social planning, 21
  and social work, 14, 15, 16, 26, 59,
    61, 78
  socialist, 4, 34, 35, 40, 41
  socialist practice, 5, 96, 98
  socialist theory, 96, 98
  and the state, 12, 15, 20, 22, 27, 35,
    39, 49, 85, 92, 98
  and struggle, 46
  as tasks, 34
  theory, 4, 5, 14, 19, 31, 32, 37, 40,
    46, 103
  theory and practice of, 32, 46, 64, 78,
    96, 97
  training, 77–83, 94
  values, 5, 48, 90, 99
  and the urban programme, 15, 16–18,
    85
  and the voluntary sector, 19, 23, 27,
    50, 55, 71, 85, 87, 88, 93
  and the welfare state, 23, 25, 26, 27,
    97
  and women, 3, 11, 20, 37, 41, 66, 69,
    75–7, 90
  and youth work, 16, 79

community workers
  background of, 75–7
  dilemmas in work, 22, 99
  experiences of black, 75–6, 77
  as managers, 94
  as professionals, 40
  role of, 65
  in the statutory sector, 85, 92
  in the voluntary sector, 85
Convention of Scottish Local
    Authorities, 75, 78, 82, 83
co-operation, 34
Craig, G., 3, 5, 11, 14, 26, 65
Croft, S., 58
Curno, A., 20, 65, 69
Curno, P., 65

Dixon, G., 66, 69
Dominelli, L., 5, 8, 21, 59, 60, 66, 67,
    69, 71, 90
Dunleavy, P., 48

economy, 22, 23
Educational Priority Area Projects, 63

Fairbairn – Milson Report, 16
Federation of Community Work
    Training Groups, 77, 78, 80, 81,
    82
feminism, 37, 41, 65
feminist community work, 66
  definition of, 67
  processes in, 68
Foot, P., 16
Francis, D., 6, 26, 72, 75–6, 83, 85, 92,
    93
Freeman, J., 68, 93
Freire, P., 52, 63–4, 73, 102, 103

Gamble, A., 26
Giarchi, G., 6
Glasgow rent strike, 11
Glenn, A., 75–6, 92, 94
Goetschius, G., 4, 33
Gough, I., 9, 35, 98
Gramsci, A., 43–6, 98–9, 103
  analysis of community work, 45
  analysis of social movements, 44
  and change, 46
Green, J., 18, 20
Greenham Common, 52, 67
Griffiths Report, 59

Hadley, R., 26, 59
Hall, S., 24, 51
Hanmer, J., 37, 67, 68
Hatch, S., 59
Heginbotham, C., 58
Henderson, P., 6, 33, 34, 36, 65, 89, 90,
    91
Holmes, J., 76, 77
Hutton, W., 29

imperialism and community work, 7–8,
    60
Ingleby Report, 16
inner cities, 16–19, 27

Jacobs, S., 5
Jacques, M., 51
Jeffs, T., 76, 79
Jones, D., 14, 59, 61, 65
Joseph, K., 18

Kettle, M., 15
Kuenstler, P., 14
Kuper, B., 76, 79

labour movement, 8, 13, 22, 36, 65
Labour Party, 3, 13, 35
Leaper, R.A.B., 33
Lees, R., 5, 23, 65
London Weekend Return Group, 22, 35,
    66, 98
Loney, M., 7, 17, 19, 59
Lovett, T., 63, 73
Lowe, S., 48, 49

McGrath, M., 59
Manpower Services Commission, 24, 26,
    27
maintaining the status quo, 46
Marris, P., 62
Martin, I., 63
Mayo, M., 5, 8, 18, 20, 23, 65, 69, 100
Mills, R., 20
miners' strike, 22
  women's involvement, 67
models of community work, 55, 99
  black and anti-racist community
    work model, 69
  community action model, 65
  community care model, 55, 100
  community development model,
    60–1, 100

community education model, 62
community organization model, 58
feminist community work model, 66
social planning model, 61
Morris, H., 11, 63
Morris, W., 2

National Childcare Campaign, 67
National Federation of Community
Organisations, 77
National Houseworking Group, 67
National Unemployed Workers
Movement, 11, 12
National Vocational Qualifications, 80
National Women's Aid Federation, 67
National Youth Agency, 78, 80
New Right, 22, 24–6, 58, 97
new social movements, 48, 50, 51, 52
definitions of, 51
political philosophy, 51

Ohri, A., 5, 39, 66, 71, 72

Parker, R.A., 58
Pickvance, C., 49
Plowden Report, 16
pluralism, 4, 32, 39, 40
Popple, K., 39, 43
post-war consensus
decline of, 22, 35
poverty, 14
Powell, E., 16
prefigurative work, 51
Presley, F., 5
privatization, 25
Programme of the Reform on the Law
of Soliciting, 67
public sector
cuts in, 23, 26, 29

race, 16, 21, 38, 71
and poverty, 25
radicalism, 4, 18, 34, 41
Rape Crisis Centre, 67
Rée, H., 12, 63
Rimmer, J., 9
Roberts, L., 66
Rogers, V., 5, 63
Ross, M., 14
Rothman, J., 61
Rowbotham, S., 11, 20, 38, 51, 67
Ruskin, J., 2

Saunders, P., 49–50
Sayer, J., 5, 45
Scarman Report, 27
Scott, A., 48, 51
Scott, D., 80
Scottish Vocational Qualifications, 80
Seebohm Committee, 15
settlements, 7, 9, 10, 12, 27, 97, 98
Shelter, 19, 98
Simon, R., 45
Skeffington Report, 16
skills in community work, 27, 33, 89–91
slum clearance, 35
Smith, M., 14, 76
social movements, 46–53, 102
social planning, 21, 61
role of, 62
social work, 26
and community care, 59
and community development, 61
history of, 11, 14, 15, 16
the state and community work, 12,
15, 20, 22, 27, 35, 39, 46
training, 78
socialism, 4, 34, 35, 40, 41
Solomos, J., 17, 27, 69, 70
Sondhi, R., 5, 29, 70

Taylor, A.J.P., 13
Taylor, M., 5, 29, 40
theory
and community work, 32, 34, 35, 39,
40, 78, 96
social construction of, 32
Thomas, D.N., 4, 13, 14, 15, 21, 32, 33,
34, 36, 61, 66, 69, 75, 79, 83, 85,
89, 90, 91, 92, 93
Tönnies, F., 2
Toynbee, A., 9
Training and Enterprise Councils, 28
training in community work, 77, 94
college-based, 78–9
field-based, 79
strengths and weaknesses, 81
vocational, 80
Twelvetrees, A., 4, 22, 33, 39, 60, 61,
69, 89

Urban Development Corporations, 85
Urban Programme, 15, 16–19, 85, 87,
88
urban social movements, 48, 49, 50, 52

voluntary sector
  black, 70, 71, 87
  funding of, 87, 88, 93, 94
  history of, 17
  management of, 93–5
  role of, 12, 13, 17, 19, 23, 26, 27, 50,
    55, 85, 87

Waddington, P., 7, 19, 23, 29, 36
Wages for Housework, 67
Wagner Report, 59
Walker, A., 25, 58
Ware, V., 38
welfare state, 13, 23, 25, 26
  and capitalism, 35, 97
  and community care, 58
  and the private sector, 26
  and racism, 39
  and the voluntary sector, 26
  and women, 58
West Indian Standing Conference, 70

Whitting, G., 17, 87
Williams, R., 3
Wilmott, P., 4, 14
women
  and community care, 58
  and community work, 3, 11, 20, 37,
    41, 66–9, 75–7, 90
  and poverty, 25
Women Against Violence Against
  Women, 67
Women's Liberation Movement, 20
Women's Therapy Centre, 67
working class
  community, 11, 14
  culture, 3
  struggle, 36, 46, 49

Younghusband, E., 14, 15
youth work, 16, 79
  college-based training of, 79
  field-based training of, 79

COMMUNITY PROFILING
AUDITING SOCIAL NEEDS

Murray Hawtin, Geraint Hughes, Janie Percy–Smith with Anne Foreman

Social auditing and community profiles are increasingly being used in relation to a number of policy areas, including: housing, community care, community health, urban regeneration and local economic development. *Community Profiling* provides a practical guide to the community profiling process which can be used by professionals involved in the planning and delivery of services, community workers, community organizations, voluntary groups and tenants' associations. In addition it will provide an invaluable step-by-step guide to social science students involved in practical research projects.

The book takes the reader through the community profiling process beginning with consideration of what a community profile is, defining aims and objectives and planning the research. It then looks at a variety of methods for collecting, storing and analysing information and ways of involving the local community. Finally it considers how to present the information and develop appropriate action-plans. The book also includes a comprehensive annotated bibliography of recent community profiles and related literature.

Contents
What is a community profile? – Planning a community profile – Involving the community – Making use of existing information – Collecting new information – Survey methods – Storing and analysing data – Collating and presenting information – Not the end – Annotated bibliography – Index.

208pp   0 335 19113 4 (Paperback)

COORDINATING COMMUNITY CARE
MULTIDISCIPLINARY TEAMS AND CARE MANAGEMENT
John Øvretveit

This book is about how people from different professions and agencies work together to meet the health and social needs of people in a community. It is about making the most of different skills to meet people's needs, and creating satisfying and supportive working groups. It is about the details of making community care a reality.

The effectiveness and quality of care a person receives depends on getting the right professionals and services, and also on the support given to the person's carers. Services must be coordinated if the person is to benefit, but coordination is more difficult with the increasing change, variety and complexity of health and social services in the 1990s. This book challenges the assumptions that services are best coordinated by multi-professional and multi-agency teams, and that community care teams are broadly similar. It demonstrates when a team is needed and how to overcome differences between professions, and between agency policies and philosophies.

Drawing on ten years of consultancy research with a variety of teams and services, the author gives practical guidance for managers and practitioners about how to set up and improve coordination and teamwork. The book combines practical concerns with theoretical depth drawing on organization and management theory, psychology, psychoanalysis, sociology, economics and government studies.

Contents
Introduction – Needs and organization – Markets, bureaucracy and association – Types of team – Client pathways and team resource management – Team members' roles – Team leadership – Decisions and conflict in teams – Communications and co-service – Coordinating community health and social care – Appendices – Glossary – References and bibliography – Index.

240pp   0 335 19047 2 (Paperback)

THE DEVELOPMENT OF SOCIAL WELFARE IN BRITAIN

Eric Midwinter

This textbook is aimed at undergraduate and diploma students across a wide range of the social sciences, with particular reference to those preparing for or involved in careers in social and public administration. It provides, in compact and accessible form, the story of social provision from medieval times to the present day, systematically examining major themes of:

- the relief of poverty and social care,
- healthcare and housing,
- crime and policing,
- education.

With the rise of the welfare state, and its current questioning as a chief focus, the book sets out to analyse how the state has responded to the social problems that have beset it. Consideration is given to comparative elements in Europe, North America and elsewhere, together with specific reference to issues of race, ethnicity and gender. A specially prepared glossary completes what is a well-packaged review and description of the growth and present disposition of the full range of social and public services in Britain.

Contents

Preface: How best to use this book – Introduction: Social casualty and political response – Medieval life and welfare – The nation-state and the money-economy – Industrialism's impact and the initial response – Piecemeal collectivism: Precursors of the welfare state – The silent revolution of the 1940s – The Butskellite consensus (c.1951–1973/9) – The questioning of the welfare state – General advice on further reading – Glossary of terms – Index.

208pp   0 335 19104 5 (Paperback)   0 335 19105 3 (Hardback)